# A Journey to Forgiveness

**Cindy Skimming**

1

ISBN 13: **978-0692910344**
Library of Congress Control Number: **2017912079**
**Cindy Skimming, Vernal, Ut**

# Contents

# Acknowledgments

This book is written in honor of Yeshua (Jesus), my Lord and Savior.

Special thanks to my husband, Richard, whose support made this book possible.

Thank you also to the members of my family and dear friends who believe in this venture.

# Introduction

Welcome to a step-by-step look at receiving forgiveness for ourselves and giving forgiveness to others.

Unique to this book are the following:
- The Hebrew spelling of Jesus's name is "Yeshua." "Jesus" is the Greek spelling and in these pages is enclosed in parentheses.
- This book is designed for use by individuals or by small study groups. When using it in small groups, look for the asterisk (*). This symbol indicates areas calling for sharing with one another in open dialogue.

I've noticed many hurting people in a hurting world. I have been blessed to have met a variety of people who encouraged the writing of this book. Talking with these same people on a consistent basis for over a year changed my life. This book is just one work through which my hope is that everyone who reads it will be blessed. With the encouragement of several individuals who wanted to see *A Journey to Forgiveness* completed and in circulation, I have now finished.

This is a step-by-step writing on the subject of forgiveness. While reading the book, you and I will be on a journey. We begin our travel quite enjoyably. Along our excursion, an event or several events take place that interrupt and change our course. Our trip has gone from traveling in pleasant weather to struggling through a snowstorm.

During the snowstorm, we will encounter a variety of obstacles that block our path to forgiveness. One interruption during our journey is learning how to deal with areas where we may get stuck, just like being stuck in a snowstorm. One example of the barriers we will face is learning how to deal with well-meaning people who are just that—well-meaning—but not helpful in moving us toward forgiveness. Other hindrances include things like our attitude.

The frame of mind leading to statements such as "I can't forgive—I just can't!" impacts the ability to forgive. Another mind-set says, "I'll *never* forgive." Another might be one of "I *won't* forgive. My answer is no." We will have specific strategies at our disposal to clear the obstacles and allow us to continue our journey. Sometimes major blockages can impede our way, such as an avalanche. Moving an avalanche out of our path can be a significant challenge. But how to get from the frigid cold temperatures of unforgiveness to the pleasant temperatures of forgiveness is what this book is all about.

Not only will we acquire the abilities and knowledge to forgive but we will also be able to go further on our journey. As with any travels, the road is not always easy. The trip may become a bit bumpy or uncomfortable along the way. It's important to realize, though, that bumps and potholes are just part of the road we must travel on.

By completing the guidelines outlined in this book, we can free ourselves from bitterness and unhealthy anger. We will have a clear understanding of what forgiveness is—and what it is not. Success awaits us at the end of our travels. Learning these techniques will not only benefit us as individuals but also those with whom we have contact in our lives.

Places exist where we will have common ground to share, and we will understand where each of us is coming from. As our stories unfold, we may be able to empathize with the person or persons involved but not be able to fully grasp the range of feelings since we personally have not had to deal with a particular situation. This will in no way hinder our growth toward forgiveness. Maybe a few differences in our journey can be shared openly with others. By participating, we can discover new approaches to changing our positions regarding forgiveness that we've not thought of before. Forgiveness is one subject a large majority of people, myself included, will be confronted with at some point in their lives to a small or large degree.

The ability to receive and give forgiveness can occur for every life. For everyone reading this book, forgiveness will be more than just words on a page. Emotions will be experienced, and the road to healing will come. Our life will be enhanced as we unlock the biblical secrets revealed in the Word of God regarding forgiveness.

Welcome to everyone who yearns to complete this journey. Items needed are a Bible, a tablet to jot down any notes that come to your attention, and a pen or pencil to draw thermometers and to mark specific spots on them. Although this is a journey we will do together, it is also an individual journey, because every person has individual situations. Each story is unique to every person involved. By completing our trip, we will not only become more forgiving people but may find ourselves possessing newfound abilities to agape love our enemies and beyond.

# Chapter 1

## Life before the News

Many of us have lives that we are comfortable with. In comparison to a thermometer, we would probably mark the temperature somewhere between sixty-five and seventy-five degrees Fahrenheit. This simply means we have a good life. That is not to say we have a perfect life. Few people have an absolutely perfect life in every area of existence, but we do have a good life. Many have a family with few conflicts, solid friendships, good health, a nice home, a dependable vehicle, and a good job. While our job pays for our lifestyle, we are then freed up to concentrate on the day-to-day activities of living.

An active lifestyle is made up of many components. Getting children ready for school, planning for a girls' night out or a vacation, baking cookies when children arrive home, going shopping, exercising, preparing for the next hunting trip, repairing a vehicle, going to a meeting to handle a big business deal, deciding what to prepare for dinner, and so on are just a few activities that keep life in motion. For now, draw a thermometer, and mark where you are or were at with life before "the News"—information that will or has impacted several areas of your life, if not every area of your life, with the added component of requiring you to forgive someone. The mark you place on the thermometer at this point likely indicates that life is worth getting up for the next day. You know you are feeling good as you step outside to greet a beautiful day with blue skies and warm temperatures. Perhaps you will go for a walk on the beach. Maybe you will join a friend for coffee or lunch. Or possibly you will discover a good book to read. Whatever that thermometer reading is means that life for you at this point is agreeable for you.

**\*For Small Groups**

Give everyone an opportunity to discuss life before "the News."

o   What season was this time of life—spring, summer, winter, or fall?

o   What specific hopes and dreams were being contemplated?

# Chapter 2

## Receiving the News

"The News" refers to an event or several events that impacted your life in several areas, which can include spiritual, mental, sometimes physical, emotional, and financial upheaval. The way we receive the News can come in many forms, such as a phone call, a knock on the door by a stranger, a personal visit from a friend, gossip through the grapevine, or perhaps a letter, an e-mail, or a text.

The News that comes in from whatever source will usually result in heartbreak. Here are just a few examples of such announcements: an unexpected death, an illness, a job loss, a divorce, the loss of a beloved pet, a severed limb, the loss of innocence, a broken trust, a loss in finances due to a plunging stock market, or being swindled by a family member or a friend.

In short, what the News means for us is that we now have to say goodbye to at least a portion of our life that has been agreeable—even when we don't want to say goodbye. We never wanted to say goodbye to that part or several parts of our lives that have brought us joy but which are now causing of brokenheartedness. Not only do we have to say goodbye but on top of everything else, we are now confronted with the whole issue of forgiveness, which can cause our thermometers to plummet from a pleasant sixty-five to seventy-five degrees Fahrenheit right down to zero and below. We find ourselves in a freezing-cold climate. This temperature drop is the first thing we will look at and begin to understand.

From an enjoyable seventy-five degrees, the temperature will decrease. As it plummets downward, a storm will eventually come in, resulting in anything from a minor snowfall to a major avalanche through which we cannot pass without help. Aid usually comes in the form of a snowplow, a snow shovel, or—at the very least—a bucket. We now have two thermometers to draw and deal with: one represents our quality of life taking a drop, and the other represents where we are on a forgiveness scale.

Sometimes we may slide off the road and just become stuck in the snow. At times like these, we may need help in order to move on. In a major snowstorm, we may have to pull off the road or spend some time at an inn or restaurant until we can see clearly once again. If you haven't already, draw two thermometers. On one thermometer, mark the place that represents the temperature that corresponds to your quality of life. On the second thermometer, mark the spot relating to where you are in forgiving someone or several people who brought devastating consequences to your life. Your honesty is needed here.

The low end of the scale (zero or below) means, "I cannot forgive," and the high end (seventy-five degrees) means, "I can forgive. I am excited to pray, forgive, and do good to someone who at one time brought desolation and ruin to my life." It is important to mark the thermometers to represent where you are right at this moment.

So, just how do we get from zero and below on a thermometer (meaning, "I'll never forgive") to an agreeable temperature of seventy-five and higher in the forgiveness realm? Continue reading. Begin to reclaim your life, and welcome joy once again.

**\*For Small Groups**

Give all participants an opportunity to discuss their thermometers and how they marked them.

# Chapter 3

## Well-Meaning...but Not Helpful

Before we begin to head toward warmer temperatures, we need to bring a couple more situations to the thermometer.

One is in the arena of being swindled. You suffered losses while the person(s) who swindled you is up skiing on the slopes or taking a vacation in the Bahamas. This will cause a further drop in temperature on your thermometer. Something else will drop the temperature as well.

Have you ever heard well-meaning family and friends say, "You have to forgive those who have hurt you, or you won't be forgiven yourself. That's in the Bible"? Family and friends are saying this to hurry you through the process of forgiveness, because seeing the pain in your life is difficult for them to witness. Painful emotions are uncomfortable to see in those we love. Another reason family and friends say this is when one or more of them are guilty of bringing pain into your life. They want you to expedite your feelings so they can feel at ease with themselves once again. When you aren't able to completely forgive from the heart at this time, they accuse you of not being forgiving. Oops—another drop in temperature! Where someone is accusing you of unforgiveness, that person's welfare is of more concern to him or her than your healing.

Another reason people say the above phrase is that they don't want you to look bad as a Christian or a believer. When people are perceived as unforgiving, this is one of the first phrases some Christians repeat—and this is where you have a high probability of getting stuck, just like being stuck in the snow. Why? Because now, on top of everything else, you get a sense of being betrayed by none other than Yeshua (Jesus) Himself.

Here is an example of a one-sided discourse: "Are you kidding me, Lord? I had to hear the News. I had to deal with the consequences. I have to deal with my feelings and the feelings of others. I suffered the losses while they were off living the good life, and now You're saying I won't be forgiven if *I* don't forgive? Why don't You just bury me in an avalanche right here and now?"

Added to this is the sense of letting the Lord down. These are the worst temperature drops so far! Place a mark on one of your thermometers representing the one-sided conversation. Are you feeling buried in an avalanche? Let's begin by digging out.

What is that I hear? The first rumble of a snowplow headed our way! As we look at the above conversation and read the upcoming verses, the one-sided dialogue will come into perspective. We will learn what was said and what wasn't. Please read Matthew 6:14–15.

Yeshua (Jesus) basically said, "Forgive, and you'll be forgiven. Don't, and you won't." Let's clear up some misconceptions concerning what He said.

Misconception number one is that His statement is a command. Some claim that what He said *is* a command. But His statement is actually just a consequence of not doing something, not a command, much like a parent saying to a child, "Do your homework, or you can't go to your friend's birthday party." The child is not *commanded* to do his homework. The child can choose not to do his homework, but then he will face the consequence of missing out on the birthday party.

Misconception number two is that Yeshua (Jesus) is unfair! Say your child came home from school with a note that read, "Johnny has three days to get an assignment done, or I will have no choice but to fail him." Fine. But you as a parent would contact the teacher to learn more about it if the teacher said, "Johnny has three days to complete his assignment, but I'm not going to give him the necessary information he needs to complete his homework. So I'll just give him an F."

Yeshua (Jesus) would never treat us this way. He does not leave us without the necessary skills or information we need to complete the assignment of forgiveness. Have you ever heard that there are no steps to forgiveness? There are. The abilities needed to make them can be learned. Only then will you be equipped to make a sound decision on whether to forgive or not. By the time you are finished reading this book, you will have the ability to forgive.

Misconception number three is that one must forgive before sunset. We will cover in a later chapter the subject of anger. Again, that's not fair if you don't know how to deal with anger at this time. Here's how to answer a well-meaning family member or a friend who approaches you about unforgiveness. Just smile and say something like, "I am caught in a major snowstorm, and it's going to take me a while to get to warmer temperatures where total forgiveness is concerned. I am a forgiving person, and I am working toward being even more forgiving."

Making a proclamation similar to the one above is important because it gives family and friends a picture they can relate to. It's not unreasonable to expect the process of raising temperatures from subzero to a pleasant seventy-five degrees to take some time. The statement also reaffirms that you are on an upward trajectory toward forgiveness in fullness and from the heart.

Next, we will consider attitudes that get us stuck in unforgiveness and how to change them.

**\*For Small Groups**

Give all participants an opportunity to discuss other attitudes that have possibly hindered or slowed their ability to forgive.

o   What are some of the feelings that arise when one is accused of being an unforgiving person?

# Chapter 4

## Feelings

Our feelings are our guides, and we would do well to listen to them and what they are trying to tell us. If we are stuck in a snowstorm, we may feel gloomy about our situation, desperate to arrive at a destination by a certain time. We may even feel fearful of running out of gas before we safely arrive at a gas station. On the other hand, we may feel exhilarated by *not* arriving at an appointment on time—we now have a legitimate excuse as to why we are not able to make our meeting.

Our feelings when dealing with unforgiveness are not to be used as excuses to block our road trip to forgiveness. Emotions are to be used as a compass, directing the steps we need to take in order to continue. Whether we have good feelings or bad toward being stuck in a snowstorm is really of no consequence. Either way, we still have to get unstuck in order to resume our travels.

The difference our feelings *can* make is whether we will smile as we figure out the best way to persevere through the storm or curse and feel unhealthy anger toward the snowstorm. Perhaps we will blame ourselves for traveling during the storm without compassion, not understanding why our feelings were formed in the first place. We eventually arrive, saying, "I can't go past this point until something is done."

We can perceive that an "I can't" attitude is viewed by many as mediocre and therefore change how we deal with this mind-set. Most people can relate to the idea that saying "I can't" is a barrier that allows us to go no farther. With this view in mind, many people give up before they start, unable to see beyond "I can't" and what that phrase is there to teach us. The attitude of giving up affects not only our own life but the lives of everyone around us.

When we say "I can't," feelings of misery are often present—and not because the choice has been made to be that way. Unhappiness exists because of a lack of knowledge and wisdom, not realizing different choices can be made. In addition, there is a lack of understanding as to *how* to be different.

This is a dilemma alcoholics often face. On the inside, he or she is screaming, "I can't handle this situation! I don't know what to do, so I'll do what I know in order to find relief from the pain I am feeling—and that is to go have a drink." To alcoholics, finding a little alleviation from the ill feelings is better than getting no relief at all, so they become willing to pay the price, even when the cost is to their detriment. The problem with this situation is that one drink leads to many more, all of which provide only temporary relief. When they are sober again, the original problem is still present, because due to lack of knowledge they haven't dealt with it. Now, in addition to what is still plaguing them, they have introduced new problems in their personal lives that impact those close to them.

But people can learn new and exciting ways to change for the better. One technique is to use the statement "I can't" to lead us to wiser choices. All we need to do is push past "I can't"—and there are ways to accomplish this. At the same time, keep the "I can't" assertion that works for our personal growth. Yeshua (Jesus) is aware and efficient in knowing when and where to say "I can't" in our favor. We can learn to do the same. The lessons "I can't" can teach us are within everyone's grasp. We can grow, change, and improve our relationship to God, ourselves, and the people we connect with. We will see these methods in action and working for our benefit. Here is a simple illustration:

Imagine standing in front of a bed of hot rocks around a campfire. Someone says, "Pick up a rock from the fire." A natural response would be, "I can't. The rocks are too hot to pick up. I'll get burned." No one would blame us for not picking up one of the rocks. Let's take this a step further. What if we were to use "I can't" to help us acquire valuable learning skills that direct us to what we *can* do? In doing so, we can make better choices because we can learn that we have choices as a starting place.

When people say "I can't," they believe that saying those words means they no longer have a choice, as if they have been robbed of being allowed to go any further—which may be the case in truth, but not always. Look at the rock-in-the-campfire illustration. We could use a tool to pick up a rock and not get burned. We could pick a rock up after the fire cooled down. We could go pick up a different rock altogether.

In the same way, we can change our lives by absorbing and applying the Word of God to our lives. Did Yeshua (Jesus) ever say "I can't"? The answer is, yes, He did. Later on, we will learn what He says of Himself and what He says of us.


**\*For Small Groups**

Give everyone an opportunity to discuss how feelings can hinder or enhance our journey toward forgiveness.

o   What are some additional choices that could be applied when dealing with hot rocks?

# Chapter 5

## I Can't Forgive

Knowing the Lord will always be fair with us is the first step to digging out from under an avalanche. Now it's time to move to the next step.

Please read John 8:28–29 and John 15:5(b). In these few short words, Yeshua (Jesus) explains what He cannot do. He cannot do anything on His own initiative, but He explains what He *can* do. He always does what is pleasing to His Father in heaven. He also reveals something about *us*: we can do nothing apart from Him. "Nothing" includes the ability to forgive. He knows this. He also tells us that we can forgive with Him—we can accomplish forgiveness with Yeshua (Jesus) and His Spirit. More on this topic appears later in the book.

He will be our strength and our guide along the way. He will see to it that we reach the destination He has mapped for us. Our achievement of receiving and granting forgiveness is not dependent on us or our abilities alone. Our success is dependent on Yeshua (Jesus) and His Spirit working in and through us. He will see us through to the end. Give Him an amen, brothers and sisters! We will soon be on our way to forgiveness and making progress during the journey, even though we still have a ways to go.

We are going to understand what we can hold on to that allows for personal and spiritual growth. We are going to learn what we no longer need to hold on to that inhibits our development. Lessons are coming up that the "I can't" mind-set can teach us. These same lessons are the same Yeshua (Jesus) has for our understanding. A person who screams, "I can't forgive him (her or them)! I just can't!" is really saying that he or she is now parked in front of an avalanche.

Have you ever seen a fallen avalanche? You're just minding your own business when all of a sudden you hear a rumbling sound. Then, before you know it, a large wall of snow blocks any further travel until the obstruction is removed. If we were to picture ourselves being physically parked in a vehicle in front of this large wall of snow blocking our path, we would be able to easily understand that no further progress is possible until the snow is moved out of the way.

A person who says, "I can't forgive! I just can't!" couldn't move forward toward forgiveness even if he or she wanted to, because too much turmoil is blocking the path on a spiritual, emotional, mental, and sometimes physical level at that point in time. Continue reading, and we will soon discover that admitting "I can't" is a great place to begin moving the avalanche out of our way.

Confessing the words "I can't" is a powerful place to begin, because three accomplishments are associated with the word "can't," and that word brings these about consistently and works every time.

The word "can't" comes with built-in boundaries. For example, if I go to a store with twenty dollars, then I *can't* purchase anything over that amount. From here, let's take it a step further. What if I were to say, "I can't marry an alcoholic." That's a healthy boundary. Wholesome boundaries are good for us; they indicate what we can't have in our lives, working in our favor and staying in line with God's Word. This is similar to the statement Yeshua (Jesus) made when He said He could do nothing on His own initiative. He had God boundaries in place.

In the Word of God, Hebrews 4:15 states that Yeshua (Jesus) was tempted as we are, but He did not sin. He was without sin due to the healthy boundaries He had in place. When we say, "I can't," one lesson to learn is that it's okay for us to have healthy boundaries when they are in place to protect us from sin.

The second achievement the word "can't" makes possible is that it shows us where we may be stuck. If I am caught in a snowstorm and can't drive through an avalanche that is blocking my way, I may need to get some help moving the snow off before I can continue. We need to be aware of areas where we feel stuck so that we don't fall into the trap of giving up, which leads to debilitating feelings about certain situations. In order to become unstuck, here the word "can't" spurs the question, "Then, what *can* I do?" The word "can't" breaks the barrier to what you *can* do, thus it has already broken up or begun to move the avalanche, because the first "I can" is built right in. Here's how it works.

People saying "I can't!" have confessed to something they cannot do at this time, but *admitting* they can't is something they *can* do—and just did! They have now broken their relationship with "I can't" and moved the relationship to the realm of "I can." With this one bit of information, the avalanche will begin to move. How? By realizing or learning what you *can* do. If you can't drive through the avalanche in front of you, then what *can* you do to start moving the snow that's blocking your path? The answers may include grabbing a shovel or calling for help.

So, let's begin. Mark your thermometer with initials, words, or small phrases that represents some of your "I can't" sentences. I'll give you some examples that may or may not apply. The point is to use your own phrases that apply to you.

- I can't get that picture out of my mind.
- I can't get over the angry words that were spoken.
- I can't get over the loss of my best friend.
- I can't get over the betrayal.
- I can't get over missing the love of my life.
- I can't get over the anger I'm feeling right now.
- I can't get over the initial shock of what happened.
- I can't handle all the losses involved. It's just too much.
- I can't handle the bankruptcy of the company.

Now that we have a list of "I can'ts," let's begin the list of "I cans." On a separate piece of paper, write down ten things you can do to deal with one of the "I can'ts." Do this for every "I can't" that you listed. I'll give some examples that may or may not apply to your situation. Write "I can" declarations that work for you.

- I can admit where I am right now.
- I can read God's Word and get some help.
- I can call a family member or a friend who can be trusted.
- I can confide in my pastor.
- I can read a book or several books about what I am facing and learn how others dealt with this situation successfully.

- I can watch a YouTube video on the subject.
- I can take a break for a while and get some fresh air, go for a walk, or attend a play.
- I can attend a seminar if there is one in my area.
- I can talk to a professional counselor.
- I can attend a small support group. If there's none available, I can start one.

And the list goes on. Now, add to this list things you can do that resonates with you. Maybe you are an artist or involved with theater. How could you use those skills in the "I can" attitude? Learning what you *can* do empowers you. At this point, the avalanche blocking the road to forgiveness will begin to move.

Let's look at the first "I can" example and ask a question. Will an alcoholic quit drinking as long as he blames or places guilt on someone else for being his reason for drinking? The answer is, not likely. Our words, actions (behaviors), attitudes, beliefs, and feelings can devastate the lives of those we interact with. The opposite is also true. Our words, actions, attitudes, beliefs, and feelings can also greatly enhance their lives. We as a people love life when we are able to enhance the lives of others. At the same time, we don't want to own up to our responsibility when we create havoc in their lives.

When we do not accept our own words, actions, attitudes, beliefs, and feelings and place blame, guilt, or anger on someone else as our reason for behaving or believing a certain way, we throw away our power to make positive changes for ourselves and those around us.

Here's an example of throwing away our power versus keeping it. Have you ever heard a statement like, "He makes me so mad when he drinks." Here's the problem. As long as the person doesn't stop drinking, the person angry with the situation is powerless to make a positive change and gets stuck in anger. Now, let's look at keeping our power by saying something like, "I feel angry when he drinks because I have seen firsthand what the abuse of alcohol does to people." Confessing and owning anger in the above example and owning having a problem with drinking now opens the door to considering some healthy ways of dealing with the anger and the drinking. Let's look at the story of Jonah for a moment.

In the story of Jonah, a great storm arises at sea. A whole crew, along with the ship and Jonah, are in jeopardy. The crew asks Jonah several questions, and then they ask a big one: "What in the world are we supposed to do to you so that the sea might calm down for us?" The crew asked this because the storm was getting worse. Now, look at Jonah's response: "Pick me up and throw me overboard, and then the sea will calm down for you. I know that because of me, this big storm has come upon you." The crew didn't want to do that, and the story continues, but here's the point in this part of the story: Jonah accepted his actions and words as the reason for the crew's predicament and took responsibility for how to correct the situation. He kept his power, and he knew what he needed to do. He also didn't cast blame, become angry, or place guilt on the crew for something he himself had done.

Jonah could have taken the route of accusing the crew of not having been smart enough to get to shore before the storm broke out. He could have blamed them for not being experienced enough to get them safely to shore once the storm had begun. He didn't. He simply stated that the storm was jeopardizing everyone because of something he himself had done, and the necessary steps were taken to calm the storm for everyone else aboard the ship.

So, let's see where we're at in beginning to move the avalanche out of our way.

**\*For Small Groups**

Give everyone an opportunity to discuss "I can't" and "I can" attitudes and how each can assist us.

o   What feelings surface when we bring good experiences to the lives of others?

o   What feelings surface when others bring good experiences into our lives?

o   What feelings might we experience when we bring painful experiences into the lives of others?

o   What do we feel when others bring painful experiences into our lives?

o   What is most challenging when owning up to our responsibility for bringing havoc into the lives of others?

o   What are some methods to deal with our responsibility that are revealed in the Jonah story and that we could apply to our lives?

# Chapter 6

## I Won't Forgive—the Answer Is No

There is a big difference between "I can't" and "I won't." Confessing "I won't forgive" is all-out defiance and disobedience to Yeshua (Jesus) as Lord of our life. But He understands the feelings and the causes behind this disclosure, and He has the solution.

We need look no further than His Word for His remedy and trust His guidance as to where He may send us. Simply put, He understands what few others do—and on even deeper levels than we ever will. Using a statement like the one above often leads to a place to end a conversation by pointing out the person's error in not being obedient to Yeshua (Jesus) as Lord. Instead of closing a door, though, which keeps a person stuck in a state of unforgiveness, we are going to open the door toward forgiveness.

We will discover reasons for the emphatic stand of "I won't" and have strategies in place to aid in changing them. The answer may start out as "I won't forgive," but that same answer can change to "I am willing" by the time we are finished. Before we begin, each of you is encouraged to make your stories personal to you. You will need a sheet of paper and something to write with. You will find that you have a treasure trove of discoveries about what is blocking your path to forgiveness. You will also find specific suggestions that may work for you in healing those areas. At the very least, you will be pointed in the right direction to continue.

I'll give you some examples—some may resonate with you, and some may not. Some illustrations may not even be listed. If they aren't, you can go ahead and list them. We will be building a small town, leading each of us to our personal healing. Our path toward forgiveness will become evident. You may find that during your journey, the answers you discover will help not only yourself but multitudes of others.

Does the word "multitudes" sound familiar? It will when you think about it. Yeshua (Jesus) fed over five thousand people. He began with very little, and so can you. Can you picture yourself writing a book, helping others with struggles you have already overcome? If not, perhaps you can see yourself speaking to groups of people and relaying valuable insights that aid others. The Lord has given you gifts and talents with which to bring Him glory. You probably have a good idea what they are, but if not, ask those who know you well.

The Lord's Word teaches us not to look only to our own interests but also to the interests of others. What He means is this: we are not to look to our own interests at the expense of others. Nor are we to look to the interests of others at our own expense. We are to consider the interests of both. This concept is discussed in 2 Corinthians 8:12–14. Some confusion exists about looking to the interests of others as being more important than ours. If we combine those statements with the statements in 2 Corinthians, we discover that we are to do that, as we are prepared in our hearts to esteem others more highly than ourselves. We will take a more in-depth look at this in a later chapter. Just know for now that you are gifted, and each person is to use those gifts for His glory.

Yeshua (Jesus) has given us abilities to share and help others along the way. My home is open to provide people with the occasion to share their gifts on a regular basis. My life is blessed during the times we come together. I look for gifts people easily embrace and are gifted with as well as those they want to embrace, even if they are not good at exercising that particular gift. The Lord is happy with them, and so am I.

While we consider ways to be useful to the Lord where we are right now, we will also look at obstacles and how to overcome them in the little town we are about to build.

How does someone overcome an obstacle? First, by recognizing there is one. As long as we cannot see a hindrance in our path, we will not see the need for a solution. Next, we need to consider the best course of action for removing the blockage. In the situation of an avalanche blocking our path, how are we to deal with it to gain the most benefit for our lives? Let's consider a few options.

We could blow it up with dynamite if we had any. Would this be beneficial to us when we realized that by blowing it up, we killed someone on the other side? We could call for help. What would we do if no one could hear or if we couldn't get a signal out to make a phone call? We could wait. Do we have the necessary supplies to wait until help comes? Could we turn around and have enough gas to arrive at a different destination? With so many choices, we must look for the ones that provide the most advantage to ourselves and others.

If we find ourselves in the temperature zone of "I won't forgive" or "The answer is no," grab a bucket. We're going to start tearing down the avalanche by building a town of igloos.

**\*For Small Groups**

Give everyone an opportunity to discuss the compassion of Yeshua (Jesus) to understand us on levels of our lives few others can.

o What ideas come to mind in assisting others using the gifts God gives?

o Were attitudes passed down to esteem others more than ourselves, even to our detriment?

o Was a frame of mind passed down to appreciate ourselves at the expense of someone else suffering pain and loss at our hands?

o What are some suggestions we can use to esteem both ourselves and others?

o How important is recognizing barriers that may prohibit our journey?

# Chapter 7

## The Town of Igloos

Welcome to the Town of Igloos. During our stay here, we will gather vital information that will point us to specific areas of our lives that may need attention. We will win victories in this little town that will allow us to resume our trip to forgiveness. We will recognize areas where we may find ourselves stuck and acquire the intelligence necessary to get free. Sadness is also part of the experience while in this town, but combined with hope, we will continue moving forward. We have several reasons for visiting the igloos. The igloos help prevent our getting stuck in despair and give us the courage to continue on our journey.

Some people never find their way out of despair and resort to suicide. I have a friend who lost his wife and a dear friend of many—myself included—to illness. A few months later, he also lost his daughter. She had taken her life. Several of us knew that his daughter was grieving the loss of her mother, but none of us were aware of just how much she was suffering. The time of year didn't help either, as May, the month of Mother's Day, was at hand. She had watched mother-and-daughter lunches taking place and was overwhelmed with seeing Mother's Day cards, flowers, and hugs being exchanged. By the end of Mother's Day, this young girl, not yet a teenager, could not get over the loss of her mother.

When we learned what had happened, all of us were saddened. The suicide was so unnecessary. I along with other women and mothers would have been delighted to take this young girl in for an adopt-a-daughter day. We all know that we could not have replaced the mother of the young girl, but we would have been pleased to have taken her shopping or to the movies. A couple of the mothers had children close to her age with whom she could have made friends. The igloos are in place to aid us.

People in the next group do not resort to suicide, but they do take an equally unhealthy route. A large number of people turn to alcohol and drugs. These results of these choices are not as quick as suicide, but they are just as deadly. Wanting pain to go away but having no knowledge of how to deal with intense emotions in a healthy environment, people just get numb. Everyone who has gone to a dentist and has had an area temporarily deadened knows that after a while, the numbness wears off, and this is what happens with people who turn to alcohol or drugs. To keep pain at a distance, more and more alcohol or drugs are needed. But the pain still hasn't gone away, and now there's even more of it to deal with.

Yet another group of people have overcome or not given in to an addiction but still get stuck. Some people take one step forward and three steps back. Like trying to rock a car back and forth to dislodge it from a place where it is stuck, they make a little progress for a little while, but before long, they find themselves back where they were. People in this group just don't make a lot of progress and do not want to advance, at least for a while. Persons in this group are easy to identify. Study a toy train set sometime. The train goes around and around on the track, stopping at different yet familiar stations. The people operating the train do not realize they can get off the train. They can take a different train to a better place.

Others recognize they are stuck and want to make progress but do not know how. Why would you take a vehicle to a mechanic to have it worked on? Because a mechanic has the knowledge needed to repair the vehicle. He discovers what is broken and fixes it. The first step in getting unstuck is to realize that we are stuck and then take the necessary steps to improve.

Yet another group of people are absolutely determined to overcome every obstacle life throws at them, and they get on with the business of living. I have a cousin who I greatly admire. A few years ago, he was involved in an accident while working on a job. He was confined to wheelchair for a long period of time. He was told he wouldn't be allowed to return to his work. He and his wife suffered hardships in their relationship. Their finances were in ruins, and they experienced the loss of their home. These two could not catch a break. I had the pleasure of interviewing him and his wife. I was curious to learn what had kept him going when he could so easily have given in to despair. He didn't just visit the Town of Igloos that we are soon going to construct; he dealt with each igloo involved. Here are some of the steps he took.

The first obstacle was the issue of his not being able to walk. One day, he just threw his wheelchair right out the front door. He was determined he would walk again, and gradually he did build his muscles up and achieved this goal. Next, he was determined to drive, so what did he do? He drilled a hole in his cast. He took the knob off his gearshift so that he could shift gears while wearing his cast.

After that, he had to deal with getting retrained for new employment. The agencies he was working with to build a new career weren't too excited about his prospects because of his physical condition. But he would not take no for an answer.

What was his outcome after everything he faced? He has a job he is very good at. He has a new home in a new location that he thoroughly enjoys. He and his wife have their relationship on the mend and in good standing. Their credit is restored. I asked a question: "What gave you the incentive to keep going?" His answer was, "I wanted my integrity back. I wanted to support my family again. That was something I hadn't done in a long time. I wanted to feel like I was contributing and being beneficial to someone as a worthwhile employee. I refused to give up!" People in this group are not just ready to move forward; they are like bulldozers moving snow out of their way, one scoop at a time.

Visiting a particular igloo can help us realize where we are or where someone we love might be. Another aid an igloo may provide is to help us understand why and how we got there. An additional help of the igloos is that they provide us with encouragement as we overcome any hindrances.

While stopping at the different igloos, make a note of the ones that speak to you. Not everyone will identify with every igloo, and that's okay. Just visiting the different igloos can deepen our sense of compassion. By the time we leave the Town of Igloos, we will be equipped with insights as to what needs our care, and we will leave the town in victory. Everyone can have triumph, large or small, with the assistance of the Lord. There is no obstacle in existence that the Lord cannot help us overcome. Where there has been betrayal, He can renew our trust in Him, in ourselves, and in others once again. Where there has been brokenness, He will be there by our side.

Yeshua (Jesus) will be with us in the Town of Igloos. This little town will consist of several small igloos, each with a name at the top.

Feel free to come up with some of your own names, but here are some to get us started: the Igloo of Brokenheartedness, the Igloo of Devastation, the Igloo of Accusation, the Igloo of Justification, the Igloo of Betrayal, the Igloo of Loss, and the Igloo of Depression.

As we prepare to leave the Town of Igloos, a discovery is made. A larger igloo, its city hall, has three separate offices. The names of the offices are "Not Fair," "Don't Deserve," and "Too Angry." Anger has several additional departments. Each will be discussed in upcoming chapters.

Suffice it to say for now that many igloos are found in the Town of Igloos. The Lord tries to talk to us about forgiving certain people who have wreaked havoc in our lives, and the answer to Him at this time is, "No! Not now! Not ever!" Several of us are not on speaking terms with the Lord on this topic; sometimes we haven't been for years! Visiting the different offices in the town's city hall with feelings of not being treated fairly is prevalent. So, why be the one asked to forgive? "They don't deserve to be forgiven" is another attitude that exists for a time. There are also feelings of anger that can inhibit forgiveness.

But after a period of time, a very small turning point is reached. For myself, the act of screaming or crying out to the Lord was crucial.

I was feeling very angry one day when I slammed His Word shut and replied, "Okay. I get it

Lord. You're not going to change Your mind. Forgiving people who have hurt me is something You want me to do. Here's what I am telling You. You had better give me a heart to forgive, because right now I don't have one. You had better teach me how, because I don't know how to forgive at this point. And forgiveness had better be real, not something phony, when we're finished."

And thus we began. We will arrive at places where we can very specifically name our igloos with our reasons for saying no. We need to name the igloos in order to recognize them and then deal with them, otherwise we will remain stuck in our igloos and unable to move on. Also needed is to be specific about what is needed from the Lord in getting to the next steps toward forgiveness. This is known as prayer. If you can't pray an honest prayer for help in forgiving someone, contact someone who can pray for you.

Calling or texting someone who can intercede on your behalf is powerful. Here's the beauty of intercessory prayer: the person you talk with doesn't even have to know the details unless this is information you want to share. What's important here is that you own your feelings of unforgiveness at this time. The person praying for you will be asking the Lord to break down and remove all blockages preventing forgiveness and asking Him to bring healing for you that will enable you to forgive.

If you need to call someone, do so. If you have already prayed, we're ready to continue.

At this time, many people are told something like, "How can you say the Lord is your Lord if you're not willing to do what He says, such as forgive someone?" Here's a word of encouragement from Yeshua (Jesus) Himself. Please read Matthew 21:28–31. These verses are very comforting to anyone who has told Him no initially but eventually did what He asked. He sees and knows the igloos we have that the world doesn't see. He also knows that to some degree, healing needs to take place in each igloo. Who knows? He may just bring healing on a Sabbath. Here, the Lord will be invited to each igloo.

**\*For Small Groups**

Give everyone an opportunity to discuss different ways people deal with volatile emotions.

o   Does everyone have a friend that can be called for assistance in prayer?

o   Do you feel safe in sharing honestly where you are with respect to forgiving someone at this time?

o   Where are other places in the Word of God where people initially told Him no but turned their response to yes?

# Chapter 8

## The Igloo of Brokenheartedness

The beginning point will be at the Igloo of Brokenheartedness. Psalm 34:18 tells us that "the Lord is near to the brokenhearted and saves those who are crushed in spirit." We will rely heavily on God, His word, and His presence. For those broken in heart and crushed in spirit, know that God is near and very close to anyone in this situation. He is extremely close to those who are experiencing the Igloo of Brokenheartedness. In this igloo, the tears are free to flow. Life doesn't make sense here, and it's not supposed to. Nothing else takes place in this igloo but allowing pain to be released. Released anguish often comes in the form of tears, but it may happen in other forms as well, like screaming into a pillow, drawing or doodling on paper in no particular form, fishing through ice, walking in the igloo, or crying with someone who can listen or cry with you.

Drawing on paper was an outlet open to my friend Sarah. The following is part of her story.

"I was sitting in my home when the news came, and tragedy had struck. For weeks after the initial shock, all I could do was pick up a pen and a paper and draw circles. Sometimes the circles were large. Sometimes they were small. Other times they just stayed in the same place, like going around on a racetrack. There were brief moments of anger where I tore the paper with my pen. Life didn't make sense to me. I couldn't unravel why tragedy had struck. I couldn't figure out who was responsible for what. This went on for months. I just sat and cried while drawing circles on paper. I was struggling just to take my next breath. I found myself striving just to survive. I didn't want to continue with life. After learning a piece of information, I was finally ready to move on. I moved to the next igloo."

Countless people's stories may identify with Sarah and her experience.

Heartache that impacts one or more areas of life is part of the Igloo of Brokenheartedness. The inability to move beyond this igloo is often due to pain not being released and accepted for what it is. The intention here is twofold. One is to find your way to relieve pain by allowing it to surface and feeling the sadness and tears that come with being broken in heart without any retaliation.

People who want us to move on will often say, "Well, you ought to be over that by now. That was twenty years ago." The problem with this type of scenario is that the person suffering will often stop the feelings from being expressed and accepted. He or she will not move on easily, if at all, in a healthy manner because the feelings are still there, waiting for someone to say it's okay to feel that way and to express them. I understand. This is where Yeshua (Jesus) really comes through for us. With Him, we are not alone and can express our pain. Finding ways to open our water spigots and let the tears fall is acceptable.

This will mark the beginning of your personal story, or perhaps several stories. When several stories are involved, just take one at a time. The second step is to release the sorrow and anxiety in a safe manner for yourself and others. You may be able to rely on a friend or a counselor.

Compassion is needed here as despair is given permission to be felt, acknowledged, and released. As to when to leave this place, it is different for everyone. You may need to visit several times. Each of us has memories. Parents who have lost children often find themselves in this igloo again after watching other children playing in a park. Many times, spouses who have lost their mates find themselves in this igloo again when seeing a couple holding hands.

The stories are different, but one truth remains: the broken heart returns. However, the duration of the visit here decreases, and the visits themselves become fewer. At the appropriate season, the time will come to move to a different igloo—the Igloo of Devastation.

### *For Small Groups

Give everyone an opportunity to discuss the Igloo of Brokenheartedness.

o   Has anyone experienced a period of time in which life did not make sense?

o   Were you ever told that "You ought to be over that by now"?

# Chapter 9

## The Igloo of Devastation

In the Igloo of Devastation, life still doesn't make
sense, but small things begin to be recognized.
There was a point in my life where nothing about
the life I knew was left intact. My entire life felt like
a home destroyed in a violent earthquake. Every
area of my existence was impacted, which included
my spiritual, mental, emotional, physical, and
financial well-being. If you have ever walked into a
home that has been demolished by an earthquake,
hurricane, or fire, you may find a piece of glass and
then ponder what the piece of glass was. A piece of
window? If so, which one? A piece of a water glass?
Where does it belong?

A life in ruins is what the Igloo of
Devastation is like. Things are recognized but
without a sense of exactly what they are and where
they belong. Life continues, and decisions need to
be made as to how to deal with the debris.

Some people choose to clear away the
broken pieces of a shattered home and rebuild. The
new homes are often larger, and life resumes once
again somewhat normally. For these people, the
Igloo of Devastation is still felt and is not
undermined.
Others handle their devastation differently—they
move away. One thing is definite about the people
who leave, though: they experience the feeling of
not belonging there anymore. Certain aspects of life
as it was will never again be restored. The
devastation is simply too great to continue. A
normal life will not return. People in this group
have made a decision not to place themselves or

their families in the position of possibly having another earthquake wipe out their lives again. It is time to move on in a new direction.

Countless families were faced with this same situation dealing with dustbowl disasters in the 1900s. The Great Depression is another time when people were faced with difficult challenges. With no real plan as to where they would go or what they would do, they simply left as opportunities presented themselves. Some left quietly by night, and others left by day, but all left under brutal circumstances. Taking the lessons they learned with them in the Igloo of Devastation, they eventually formulated new plans for a better life in the way of a home, job, money, and friends.

When considering the Igloo of Devastation, events in our lives are not always due to a disaster like an earthquake or a fire. Many times, our lives are put into this igloo due to irresponsibility, either by our own decisions or those of other people. More often than not, the choices were a combination of ours and those of others. Messiah (Christ) identifies and understands us in this igloo as well.

Yeshua (Jesus) is intimate with the Igloo of Devastation. If He were to have had such an igloo, one of His experiences would have been when He was on the cross, His face marred beyond recognition. The accounts of His experience can be read in Psalm 22, Isaiah 50:6, and the multiple New Testament descriptions. The Lord Himself will vindicate you. Read through the Psalms and choose His healing words that apply to you, such as Psalm 9, where His Word says, "He is a stronghold for the oppressed. He does not forget the cry of the afflicted. The needy will not always be forgotten, nor the hope of the afflicted perish forever."

Ready or not, decisions made that affect our lives at this level carry us to the Igloos of Accusation and Justification.

## *For Small Groups

Give everyone an opportunity to discuss a time when life is or was devastated.

o   What did people in the group decide to do—rebuild and stay or move away?

o   Did anyone experience the feeling of no longer belonging?

# Chapter 10

# The Igloos of Accusation
# and Justification

The Igloo of Accusation is not the same as guilt over something we said, did, or continue to do. This will be discussed in a later chapter. In the Igloo of Accusation, we are accused of saying or doing something or many things we are not guilty of. Here's a short story to demonstrate.

Many have heard of the two friends and a thief. Friend one takes friend two to a store to do some shopping. Friend two asks friend one to watch over her handbag while friend two goes to the ladies' room. Friend one agrees and turns away briefly to look at a piece of clothing. While she is turned away, a thief comes along and steals the handbag. When friend two returns, she accuses friend one of not keeping her handbag safe. Friend one in return accuses friend two of not looking out for her own handbag by not taking it with her.

Who is the true culprit? The answer is the thief who took the handbag to begin with. If you want to know whether or not accusations are true of you, look at the outcome of your life.

If your life turned out to be what you were accused of, chances are the accusations are correct. If not, the accusations are not true of you. The Igloo of Accusation is still painful to deal with because accusations that are not true are harmful on spiritual and emotional levels. The Igloo of Accusation is closely related to the Igloo of Justification, where we try to justify our actions that were not good.

So, what is God's attitude toward the Igloos of Accusation and Justification? Find out by looking at both Old and New Testaments.

Let's apply His healing Word to these two igloos. In Genesis, God was in the garden with a man (Adam), a woman (Eve), and a serpent. God asked Adam a couple of questions. "Who told you that you were naked? Have you eaten from the tree that I commanded you not to eat of?" The man answered God and said, "It was the woman that You gave to me," thereby accusing both God and the woman for his own part in eating the fruit and justifying himself as to why he ate it. God turned to the woman and asked, "What is this you have done?" The woman accused the serpent for her part in eating the fruit and justified her participation. The serpent had no one to accuse. What happened next? God looked at the serpent and told him that because of what he'd done, he was going to face specific consequences for his actions. Then God did the same with the man and the woman.

The woman was going to have distinct situations to face and deal with. To the man, God said, "Because you listened to the voice (influence) of your wife and ate from the tree I told you not to eat of, here are the effects concerning your life that you will have to deal with." God executed the consequences according to the actions (behaviors) of each person involved.

God holds each of us accountable for our words, actions, attitudes, beliefs, and feelings as well as how we treat others. God will not allow accusation or justification to sway His judgments when dealing with consequences for how others have treated us or what they have said or done. He also will not allow us to accuse others or justify ourselves to sway His judgment when dealing with consequences for how we have treated others and what we have said or done. Is this true in the New Testament as well? Yes.

Please read 2 Corinthians 5:10. In short, we're all going to appear before Yeshua (Jesus), in front of His judgment seat, and be recompensed for our deeds in the body according to what we have done, good or bad. Yeshua (Jesus) takes it a step further and even holds us accountable for our words. Please read Matthew 12:36! This is good news. Everyone can leave the Igloos of Accusation and Justification by realizing what we are and are *not* accountable for. We are not accountable or responsible for things we do not say, did not say, did not do, and do not do.

Next, we'll look at the Igloo of Betrayal.

**\*For Small Groups**

Give everyone an opportunity to discuss letting go of what we are not responsible for and what that means to different individuals.

o   How do the Igloos of Accusation and Justification not work in our favor?

o   Is accountability in our dealings with others an awakening?

o   Is the thought of appearing before the judgment seat of Yeshua (Jesus) comforting based on what we have done, whether good or bad?

# Chapter 11

## The Igloo of Betrayal

In the Igloos of Accusation and Justification, we get blamed for the words, actions (behaviors), attitudes, beliefs, and feelings of others directed at us as their reasons for treating us the way they do. Not only do we get the blame; we are also held responsible for hurtful words spoken to us by others. This puts a false guilt onto our shoulders and frees others to betray us, which is the next igloo.

The Igloo of Betrayal activates when something that shouldn't have happened has fierce repercussions to our lives. Betrayal can happen through a family member, a friend, or a stranger unknown to us. The Igloo of Betrayal is difficult to be in because often we don't want to admit that we were betrayed. Betrayal comes through persons who were supposed to be trustworthy in their behavior toward us, but when all is said and done, the opposite turns out to be true. To say goodbye to the Igloo of Betrayal, some steps need to be taken.

First, a couple of questions need to be answered. One is, do you (the one betrayed) want to stay in the relationship and do the work necessary to reestablish trust? The second question is, does the one who betrayed you want to stay in the relationship and do what is necessary to reestablish trust? If both parties say yes, the road to healing, while still challenging, will be achievable.

The one betrayed will need to feel safe in setting certain boundaries about what is and is not needed from the other person, saying, "I don't need you to threaten or try to push me into trusting you again instantly. This will take time. I do need you to be more understanding." Also, the one betrayed may come up with ideas or suggestions of how trust can be rebuilt.

The same holds true for the one who betrayed. He or she may need reasonable actions from the one betrayed in order to heal his or her part and reestablish being trusted once again. The one who betrayed also needs to feel safe in setting boundaries about what is and is not needed from the other person. While many testimonies exist from people who succeed at leaving this igloo with the relationship intact, sometimes even stronger, there are also many who don't have this success story. Under these circumstances, a different path must be taken to leave the Igloo of Betrayal.

Numerous people hear words like "I knew what I doing. I knew it would hurt you, and I decided to do it anyway." A more extreme example is this, heard when a friend asked a friend of his why he was being unfaithful to his wife. His friend replied, "Because I can. All I have to do is accuse my wife of not trusting me and of being unfair. When I do that, she shuts up, and I'm free to cheat." This only worked until his wife found out. Needless to say, that relationship did not stay intact. Afterward, the husband was devastated that the relationship ended. He just never envisioned it not being there. By the time reality set in, there was no going back to try for her again. She was done.

The betrayals in the above examples are extremely painful to deal with because, to begin with, the one betrayed has to be subjected to hearing about the betrayal and then must process all the pain apart from the one who betrayed. The one who did the betraying doesn't want any part in the healing process. He or she just wants out. People leave.

There are several reasons people may not want to be involved in the healing process: true guilt; shame; anger; inability to face the devastation they have brought to the life of another; greed; and unwillingness to bear any responsibility for their part, blaming the other person and justifying themselves. Another reason may be that they want to start a new life, which means leaving the old life behind.

We don't have just the obstacles listed above to overcome. We must also overcome the painful realities of not being validated concerning our own experiences, which is difficult to go through. My heart goes out to everyone who has been shoved aside and not considered important.

Here, a question comes to the surface. How does any degree of healing take place with so many barriers surrounding one igloo? The answer is that God removes all obstacles involved, and we will soon learn how He does it. God hasn't left us without a way of finding some degree of healing concerning the Igloo of Betrayal.

We're going to look at a specific verse and break it down to learn how to apply the Word of God in dealing with this sensitive igloo. Before we come to His Word, understanding a couple of ideas will be helpful. The first concept is that something or someone can have more than one purpose. If I boil water, I can use it to make a cup of tea. I can keep the water boiling and use it to steam some vegetables. I can also use the remainder of the water to boil some eggs. The boiling water was useful for three different purposes. The same is true of people. A person can be a spouse, a father, a mother, a friend, an employer, an employee, a brother, a sister, an uncle, an aunt, and so on. One person can fill many roles.

There is a second concept to consider as well: the thought of doing something *for* another person, such as fixing a flat tire *for* someone else. The person who changed the tire did that to help another person. There is also the act of buying a gift for someone. A person purchases a gift *for* someone to brighten that person's day.

Now that we have a couple of references to go by, let's see what God's Word says. Please read 2 Corinthians 5:21.

"He (God) made Him (Yeshua, Jesus), who knew no sin, to be sin *for* us, so that in Him we might become the righteousness of God." The first information to be understood here is that the person of Yeshua (Jesus) knew no sin. In the sinless state of Yeshua (Jesus), He would not know anything about guilt, shame, or unhealthy anger toward Himself. He would not have to face any devastation He brought to the life of another through Himself, because He knew no sin. Nothing holds Yeshua (Jesus) back or is in His way. Hold on to that thought as we look deeper at Yeshua (Jesus) having more than one purpose.

The fact that He (God) made Him (Yeshua, Jesus), who knew no sin, to be sin *for* us contains within it more than one purpose. If I were to draw two lines in the shape of a cone and write the word *us* on one side and *others* on the other side, you would see a dual objective. Remember when we do something *for* someone it is to help him or her.

Yeshua (Jesus) was made to be sin *for* us, meaning not just for us as individuals but also those who have sinned against us. He can now represent the person or persons who sinned against us and thus validate our experiences and our feelings. In His sinless state, He is free to come forward in place of the ones who sinned against us and say, "I am so sorry you were sinned against." He will even name the specific sins involved. That's powerful, because in order to begin healing when addressing betrayal, our experiences and feelings need to be validated. Yeshua (Jesus) does this *for* us even when no one else will.

If not one other person ever comes forward, Yeshua (Jesus) will, and He will come every time. He understands our igloos. He understands when no one comes forward to admit having sinned against us much less cares enough to do anything about the actions or words that have been or are harmful to us.

Next, we'll take healing of betrayal to the next level. This next step in healing betrayal is learning information about the character of Yeshua (Jesus), and here it is in Revelation 19:11. In this verse, Yeshua (Jesus) is called faithful and true. These are parts of His character. In Revelation 1:5, He is also referenced as the faithful witness. Knowing His character will assist us in further healing.

The core of betrayal, to a degree, is faithlessness. Faithlessness in relationships comes through many people, including business partners, spouses, friends, family members, and strangers. Betrayal also comes in many forms, such as divulging trusted secrets. One of the worst forms of betrayal is using someone's confidences against him or her in order to further the agenda of the one confided in. Since betrayal leads to hurting people's lives, faithfulness leads to healing.

Look to everyone in your life right now, including faithful and true pets, who have faithful and true characteristics. Cherish those people, because they place a high value on the relationship between themselves and you. They consider you of high worth in their lives. Being faithful and true are the characteristics each of you bring to one another. As to new friends, consider confiding in them that a betrayal in your life has taken place. You don't have to be specific as to the details. This information can be helpful to a potential new friend, providing information about why you may need time to develop trust and discover whether or not the new friend has faithful and true intentions toward you.

As we receive healing from betrayal, the next igloo to address is the Igloo of Loss.


**\*For Small Groups**

Give everyone an opportunity to discuss betrayal.

o   Are the concepts of having more than one purpose and more than one objective easy to understand?

o   How important is it to have our feelings and experiences considered valuable?

o   When you view Yeshua (Jesus) and His characteristics of being faithful and true, do you allow Him to guide you to certain relationships?

# Chapter 12

## The Igloo of Loss

In the Igloo of Loss, struggling with this issue
without naming the specific loss or losses involved
will make moving on difficult. In this igloo, losses
take shape, and we know exactly what they are. We
can name them. Losses that might be included are
the loss of a relationship through death or divorce;
the loss of innocence, trust, or self-esteem; the loss
of a job, a pet, a home, or a limb; loss of finances;
loss of a child due to kidnapping or illness; and
many other unnamed losses. These losses can be
staggering and overwhelming at first. At this point,
we're not yet dealing with the losses to improve our
situations at this time; we're just naming them.

Without complete awareness, we do begin to
deal with some of our losses. We find a new job to
replace the one we lost. We address how to rebuild
our self-esteem or learn about how to secure a
financial future, because life continues even when
we're not ready to move forward.

When finished naming the losses, many are
ready to take the next step.

A number of layers are involved with loss.
The first is that not all losses are bad. When
someone breaks the habit of smoking, the loss of
cigarettes in a person's life is a great loss. When
someone loses excess weight and feels better, that is
a good loss. When someone pays off a debt, that is
an awesome loss.

The second layer of loss is that some losses can be
replaced with something better. The loss of a job
may lead to a better job with higher pay in a more
pleasing environment. The initial job loss was a

painful experience; however, losing the old job led to something better. Another example might be when a fishing pole gets yanked by a fish into a lake. A new fishing pole with better action or sensitivity takes the place of the old one.

The third layer of loss is that we can recover from some specific losses. In recovery from loss, it is vitally important that we be specific about the losses we want to improve so that the impact on our life is not so devastating. If a financial loss is involved, strategies are in place to help us learn how to improve or regain our financial well-being.

Defining the losses is the first step in recovering from them. This is true of several different kinds of losses. For example, help is available for people suffering a loss of self-esteem or a loss of value in themselves. Losing credit is a difficult loss, but credit can be built up again over time.

Then there is the tough loss. This is a higher level of loss than the ones previously discussed. Such losses need to be handled differently.

The tough loss occurs when recovery seems to elude us. This type of loss is usually encountered when hurtful words are spoken and harmful actions are taken or when we suffer loss of relationships that at one time brought joy to our lives. The impact of heartbreak is doubled when replaced with painful words and actions on top of losing the joy—tripled with the high value we place on the words and actions of how others have treated us. When we don't value highly what a person says about us, the impact on our lives won't be deeply affected. But when we esteem the opinions of others and what they say about us, those words and actions can have devastating consequences to our lives. Then we're faced with difficult losses to recover from.

Recognizing these strong losses is the place to begin mending. Let's begin with harmful words.

Take a sheet of paper, and divide it half. On the left side, write down harmful words that were spoken. For example, "Just leave! I never want to see or speak to you again!" Words like this will bring agony when you love and want to be with the person who spoke them. Intensify the impact of those words with the knowledge that you did not intend to hurt the person involved—in fact, that was the furthest thought from your mind. But it happened anyway. It's like saying, "I didn't mean to break the window." The problem is that the window is still broken, whether it was intended or not, and you're sent away with the sound of those words echoing in your mind and wounding the spirit. Right at this moment, a person you cared for has been hurt, and now you're wounded, too.

With the harmful words written down, let's look to words that will bring healing.

On the right side of the paper, write down words that will bring healing. We are not after just any words but words that come with authority. The words of Yeshua (Jesus) are the ones we are pursuing. So, opposite "Just leave! I never want to see or speak to you again!" write, "I will never desert you, nor will I ever forsake you" (Hebrews 13:5b). Another selection from the Word might be, "He chose us from the foundation of the world." In other words, He chose you and me forever! He will never send us away—not now, not ever.
Continue to write down healing words opposite those painful words. Next, draw a line through the painful words and saturate yourself in the healing

words of Yeshua (Jesus). At this point, the beginning of recovery is taking place. Let's take recovery to the next step.

Not only are healing words essential; an increase in our self-value is vital as well. When someone we love sends us away, our perception of our worth usually diminishes for a time. This area of life requires healing, too.

Let's consider what our value is in the heart of Yeshua (Jesus). Picture along with me for a little while having absolutely the greatest life of all. This life might include a perfect home, excellent health, movie-star potential, and whatever worldly wealth you could possibly imagine. Envision a place where everything in the world is offered. Then picture Yeshua (Jesus) having all the above laid at His feet—and He turns it all away. Why? Because of the relationship He held with His Father and the value He placed on our souls and lives. We are of extreme worth to Yeshua (Jesus). We are bought with the price of His life and blood. Read the verses in 1 Corinthians 6:20 and 1 Corinthians 7:23. Soak these truths into your being.

The next step is in healing the sense of belonging. When people are driven away by the words and attitudes of others, real rejection is experienced and felt at a very deep level. Excluding or discarding someone who loves the person telling him or her to go away comes with an excruciating high price. Part of this price is usually that people in this situation end up not only dealing with the hurtful words and attitudes of others but often also rejecting or discarding themselves. Once again, we will turn to Yeshua (Jesus) for healing.

First, accept the knowledge that Yeshua (Jesus) understands rejection on a level you and I will never face. He gets the feelings of rejection we are confronted with. In order to begin to heal this area of life, we know that we are accepted, chosen, and precious to Yeshua (Jesus.) In 1 Peter 2:4, that statement is written for all to see. There are several other verses we can reference in being chosen, such as Ephesians 1:4. Yeshua (Jesus) doesn't stop here.

Read John 9:35. In this account, a blind man had been healed. He was explaining how he was healed of his blindness, and the Pharisees put the man out (rejected him). Yeshua (Jesus) found the man. Yeshua (Jesus) likewise finds us and chooses us. Now read John 15:16. Yeshua (Jesus) doesn't stop here, either. He also makes us a promise and gives us a mission. His promise is in John 6:37, where He states He will never cast out anyone who comes to Him. When we are working toward forgiving someone or several people, that becomes one of our assignments. Notice first, however, that the blind man was healed of his blindness before his mission to testify of Yeshua (Jesus) came about. So far, we know that Yeshua (Jesus) will never leave or forsake us. We are of extreme value to Him. He has chosen us. He will never cast us out. And He has given us a mission. So, next up is finding out where we belong in order to carry out the mission.

Please read 1 Corinthians 12:14–27. I don't know what part of His body any certain person is. This I do know: that Yeshua (Jesus) has a place where every person belongs. He is going to continue to heal and empower everyone to fulfill his or her task.
Let's now take the next step up in healing. When we witness people rejecting themselves, that rejection is usually occurring because of two things operating at the same time. They have been hurt by

someone they cared about or loved, and they have said and done some things they wish they hadn't. Witnessing people rejecting themselves becomes really painful to those who didn't mean to hurt those involved. The dynamic of someone rejecting themselves is different than that of someone saying and doing things intentionally to hurt someone. This situation occurs when we didn't want to hurt a person involved, but it happened anyway. Healing has to occur in this area of the heart and spirit as well.

Here is where we will become aware of what we cannot do as well as what we can do. The realization that we cannot go directly to the person involved because he or she has sent us away becomes apparent. Maybe the person has moved away. Neither can we approach him or her indirectly, because all forms of communication will be cut off.

But there is at least one thing we can do and do every time with consistency. We can pray! We can pray to the Father that He send Yeshua (Jesus) to those we unintentionally hurt and ask Him to open their hearts and spirits to be receptive to Yeshua (Jesus). We can ask Yeshua (Jesus) to restore their sense of value and self-worth. We can ask Yeshua (Jesus) to heal the hearts and spirits that we damaged. We can ask Yeshua (Jesus) to abundantly bless and protect their lives. Then, in the resurrection, when Yeshua (Jesus) says the same to them regarding their value, we will be able to stand in agreement with Him and rejoice. Maybe we'll be able to apologize to them and let them know that's what we wanted to communicate to them before they spurned us and asked us to leave. I believe we will come to a place where we can say, "You were a true blessing to me and my life. That's why I took it so hard when you sent me away. I am sorry you were hurt by my actions." We can even pray over people we have never met or whom we briefly come into contact with when we see them struggling in this area of life. Yes, we can pray!

Tough losses can be compared to a conglomeration of rocks, mud, and minerals compressed together but which can be broken apart with a sledgehammer. Hard losses, on the other hand, can be compared to a giant slab of impenetrable hardened granite. Hard losses are considered severed losses and are very challenging to deal with. A hard loss is unlike a good loss, a recovery loss, or a tough loss—it is a permanent loss in this life. Hard losses usually come in the form of losing a body limb, facing the death of someone important in our lives, going through a divorce, or experiencing the passing of a beloved pet. Not only is this type of loss a hard loss—it results in changing our lives altogether. Life will never be the same as it was or could have been. To begin to deal with these life-changing losses, we will again turn to God's Word.

With hard losses comes deep grieving. Some people look to Ecclesiastes 3:4, where God's Word states there is a time to weep, laugh, mourn, dance, and so on. Verse 6 declares that there is a time to give something up as lost. The loss is permanent, severed in this life, and a time to grieve is apparent. With a hard loss, many things are impossible to do. We cannot reach out and touch the person who is gone. We cannot feel his or her embrace. We cannot enjoy simple activities like going out to dinner or to the movies. We cannot go on vacations together. We cannot call and expect a response. We cannot talk at the end of the day. We cannot see his or her smile. The list of what we cannot do seems never-ending. People give themselves permission and a season to mourn.

The season they choose is usually the time of year the loss took place, and they grieve for a time. People usually agree that they would not want the person(s) back in their lives if pain and suffering would never come to an end. At the same time, they agree that they continue to miss the presence, essence, and dreams that will never come to fruition because of a lost loved one. There is a time to grieve, mourn, and give up as lost. So, mourn. Mourning is acceptable, and it's okay to feel the loss.

The next step in dealing with loss involves honoring the person who is gone. To illustrate, a woman's husband has passed away. Her husband loved fishing, hunting, and the great outdoors. After her husband's death, she began to honor his memory by sending others on fishing trips they never would have been able to enjoy on their own due to financial restrictions. This widow was able to capture and retain the essence of her husband by enhancing the lives of others who love fishing as much as her deceased spouse did.

Here is another example. A husband and wife had been married for many years. In their early years, the wife crafted a handmade blanket for him. One day much later on, the woman told her husband to pull over, and she covered a man sleeping on a bench with the blanket she had made for her husband. The husband was rather put out by what his wife had done. She replied, "Don't worry, honey. I'll make you a new blanket. That man needs one right now." She was as good as her word and made her husband a new blanket. After her passing, the husband went and found someone who needed a blanket. As he gave the blanket to the person in need, he smiled and said, "Here's to you, honey. You made me a better man." The husband found a simple yet profound way to honor the memory of his wife and make a difference in society, one blanket at a time.

Consider the impact of someone who has successfully dealt with the loss of a limb. People who have prevailed over the loss of a leg or arm are an incredible blessing to others who struggle with this issue. One young lady honors the loss of her leg each time she assists someone in taking those initial first steps without the other leg. Her optimistic attitude is contagious to many, as she can already see the days ahead when someone without a leg will be driving or walking. She's a source of encouragement and compassion as natural issues of frustration, anger, and disappointment surface. If a club called the "I Won't Give Up Club" existed, she would be in it. She doesn't give up on herself. She doesn't give up on the potential of others. Another way people deal with loss is to look to the future. Not all losses last indefinitely; some are only permanent in this life.

Please read Revelation 21:4. "And He (God Himself) shall wipe away every tear from their eyes." When dealing with certain situations, He is not going to leave the act of drying your tears or mine to anyone but Himself. Some people have been taught that there are no tears in heaven. That may not be a true statement, or God would not have tears to wipe away. Perhaps He will wipe away tears on the new earth so that they will not exist in

heaven. There shall no longer be any death, mourning,
crying, or pain because the first things—those that caused the mourning, crying, and pain—have passed away.

Now, I'm not going to get into the whole argument about pets not going to heaven because they don't have a soul. But I will say this: God made a promise to dry every tear, so if a beloved pet is needed to make that happen, I wouldn't be so presumptuous as to tell God what He will or will not do in drying someone's tears. Maybe they don't go to heaven, but He could resurrect the pets on the new earth and rejoin them with someone who loved them.

We'll consider one other permanent loss in this life but eternally temporary. For many, the question of why God did or did not do something comes up, and loss is felt. When this question surfaces, we wonder why Yeshua (Jesus) didn't come through for us but did come through for someone else. For example, someone might ask, "Why did He heal that person but not someone who meant a lot to me?" or "Why did He bless that relationship, and it blossoms and flourishes, while a relationship important to me went up in smoke and ended?" We may never learn why, or we might learn why, but it may not help. Learning why might assist us in understanding, but it also brings out feelings of anger. The following story will illustrate what I mean.

A family was in their home, enjoying an evening meal. A thief came onto their property and stole the family car. During the getaway, the thief also ran over and killed the family dog and wrecked the car. Now, the family learned why the thief had stolen their car. He was escaping from the police who were pursuing him. This leads to questions directed to the Lord: "Why didn't You cause the thief to fall and break his leg before he got to our house?" or "Why didn't You let the police catch the thief before he stole our car, ran over our dog, and wrecked our car?" or "Why didn't You protect us from all this happening in the first place?" This family may or may not receive satisfactory answers to their questions. The point is that at the end of the day, because of the carelessness of someone else, the members of this family still have to grieve the loss of their beloved dog and get their wrecked car repaired. Did finding out why it happened help? No. The loss is still real and is still felt.

These are losses we have to deal with. The feelings that accompany such losses are two sides of one coin. The feeling is that of being forsaken. We might ask, "Why did You not prevent that disease from happening?" This question is one side of the coin. We may also ask, "Why did You prevent the healing of that disease?" This is the other side of the coin.

The bottom-line question is, "God, why did You forsake us in this situation? We prayed hard, believed without any doubt that You could help. We called for the elders, anointed the sick. We did and said all the right stuff. Yet here we are and right now feeling forsaken by You. Not only are we feeling forsaken, but now we also have the added burden of dealing with the loss—and a hard loss, at that."

The feeling of being forsaken is natural when we have said and done all we could, and the outcome was supposed to be different than what it turned out to be according to what we read in God's Word. His

Word states that if we do certain things, believe a certain way, pray a certain way, call on others to pray, anoint, and so on, healing will come. What if we do all that, and healing doesn't come? How do we begin to heal in these situations?

To begin to accept what has happened, we need to first know more about God's Word. His Word does speak of the topics in the previous paragraph, but He doesn't stop there, as if to say, "Period, that's it." In 1 Corinthians 15:22, His Word also says that as in Adam (the likeness of Adam) having a mortal body, all die. He doesn't stop there. He goes on to say in Messiah (Christ) the likeness of Messiah (Christ) having an immortal body, all shall be made alive.

The next step in healing is realizing that our appointment to be together with loved ones again has just not arrived yet. Yeshua (Jesus) cried out, "Why hast Thou (Father) forsaken Me?" In order to be totally forsaken, Yeshua (Jesus) would never for all eternity have been together with His Father anywhere at any time again. He felt forsaken dealing with the extreme circumstances leading up to and surrounding His death. He felt abandoned, dealing with His circumstances alone. The appointment Yeshua (Jesus) had while here on earth with us was to save us. His number-one desire after that was to be rejoined with His Father, and He was. Read all of Psalm 22, focusing in on verse 24(b). But when He (Yeshua, Jesus) cried to Him (His Father) for help, He (His Father) heard. Because of what Yeshua (Jesus) suffered, His Father gave Him everyone and everything with absolute authority in honor of His Son. Read John 20:17(a), where Yeshua (Jesus) instructs Mary not to hold on to Him because He had not yet returned to His Father.

When we suffer to the point of feeling forsaken at the hands of others, we are not abandoned by Yeshua (Jesus). Our appointment with our Father has not arrived yet, and He has treasures and honor waiting for us. The verse in 1 Thessalonians 2:19 states that we are a source of hope, a crown, a source of glory and joy of our Lord Yeshua (Jesus) at His coming. He has important crowns waiting for you and me.

Prepare to leave the Igloo of Loss and visit the Igloo of Depression.


**\*For Small Groups**

Give everyone an opportunity to discuss loss.

- o   What are some additional losses that could be named and considered good or great?

- o   What are some specific losses that you have had to face? Name them.

- o   Was loss of self-esteem, self-worth, or self-value part of the struggle brought into your life as a result of loss?

- o   Have all the categories of loss come into existence in your life? Good loss, great loss, loss replaced, tough loss, and hard loss?

- o   What are some additional ways to honor the memory of someone who was important to you who is now gone?

- o   Were areas in life dealing with loss that require further attention discovered in this chapter?

# Chapter 13

## The Igloo of Depression

In the Igloo of Depression, life is dismal, and feelings of hopelessness and of having lost our way set in. The length of time we stay in this igloo is different for everyone. We ask questions like "What's the point? Why go on? I can't find joy anymore." A depressed person is weighed down with despair. Maybe a checkup by a medical professional or a talk with a counselor trained in addressing depression is in order. When serious depression is prevalent, usually several igloos affect a person, which he or she doesn't see at the time. I'll use divorce as an illustration.

When someone announces, "My spouse left me for another person," that person has found the reason he or she believes is causing the depression, and it is. Often what they fail to see, though, are the additional igloos that come with that statement that drive sadness to a state of depression. In the case of divorce, a lot of igloos are attached, and we are going to name a few. There is the loss of a relationship that was good at one time. The Igloo of Betrayal is involved. The Igloo of Broken Trust is added to the mix. The Igloo of Self-Esteem comes into play. The Igloo of Loss in Finances also creates difficulties. The Igloo of Guilt is part of the problem. The Igloo of Anger is present.

These are just a few of the igloos brought about with divorce, but these are certainly not all of them. There is also the question of how divorce will affect children. When we are dealing with this many igloos at the same time, depression sets in because we're simply overwhelmed. There are reasons for depression. There are also solutions for depression. We need to discover the initial statement but not stop there.

Write down an initial statement linked to depression when struggling with this topic. The next step is to identify the additional igloos attached. Once we have that information, we have a place to start. Under your sentence, write down all the issues connected to what you wrote down. Here, we need to focus so that we're not scattered trying to deal with so many things at once. Since this is your story, write down one to three areas you think or feel you need to work on first.

A wise choice when possible is to choose no more than three to begin to heal or grow in. For example, if you are thinking of beginning a new relationship, then an area you may choose to work on is how to rebuild trust. As headway in the area of trust progresses, another topic of growth may be how to have a better relationship so the risk of divorce isn't as high.

Let's say you are not looking to be involved with anyone soon. The areas you choose to grow in will be different. You may wish to deal with raising your self-esteem, improving the financial situation, getting a job, and so on. As healing continues in each of the issues that lead to depression, the depression will lift or at least subside.

If depression continues to hold strong, I encourage people to get the help they need. There are just too many heartbreaks in this life and impossible to cover every one of them in this book. To name just a few, there are issues of the kidnapping of a child, child abuse, sexual abuse, spousal abuse, the murder of someone close to you, suicide, and pastoral abuse where pastors have been wounded. The list of specific wounds is very long. The word of wisdom is that there is nothing new under the sun in the realm of brokenness. Whatever someone is facing, someone else has already dealt with the issue and has laid the groundwork toward healing.

Continuous sorrow without relief leads to a joyless life. Get the help needed so the feeling of being happy can return and be a part of your life once again. At some point in the Igloo of Depression, someone might very well bring up the topic of forgiveness, and we are catapulted straight into the city hall offices of "Not Fair," "Don't Deserve," and "Too Angry." These departments need to be addressed in order to maintain a forward motion toward forgiveness. For those of you who have been jolted out of the Igloo of Depression and ushered into the City Hall of Igloos, specific offices will be visited next.

Before we begin, recap lessons our trip toward forgiveness has given us thus far.

- **Remember that the Lord will always be fair with you.**

- **Use the words, "I can't" to**
  - ✓ **set healthy boundaries,**
  - ✓ **realize places that cause you to be stuck, get the necessary help, and discover what you *can* do, and**
  - ✓ **own your own words, actions (behaviors), attitudes, beliefs, and feelings, empowering you to change.**

- **Use statements to open doors that lead to forgiveness.**

- **Discover your personal treasure trove.**

- **Discover your own path.**

- **Use your gifts and abilities to glorify the Lord.**

- **Consider options.**

- **Use the Town of Igloos to make you aware of what needs care.**

- **Use the Igloo of Brokenhearted to release pain in a safe environment with acceptance.**

- **Use the Igloo of Devastation for the Lord to vindicate you.**

- **Use the Igloos of Accusation and Justification to be free of what we are not accountable or responsible for.**

- **Use the Igloo of Betrayal to rebuild trust.**

- **Use the Igloo of Loss to identify specific losses as a guide to what needs your attention.**

- **Use the Igloo of Depression as a guide to overall healing, discovering unseen igloos, and beginning to address them.**


**\*For Small Groups**

Give participants an opportunity to discuss what has stood out for them individually so far from the above list.

o   Has anyone been in the Igloo of Depression?

o   What helped in leaving this igloo?

o   Have you known someone dealing with despair?

- When depression comes, is the ability to see additional igloos present?
- Once a particular igloo is identified as needing attention, what are some strategies that can assist in coping?

# Chapter 14

## The City Hall Office of "Not Fair"

In the City Hall of Igloos, the offices of "Not Fair," "Don't Deserve," and "Too Angry" reside. We will explore the office of "Not Fair" in more depth shortly. But first, let's take a look at a couple of examples of where we may initially feel that something is unfair but where in reality, as the story unfolds, we see that fairness is indeed present.

I'll once again use the birthday party to demonstrate. When a parent tells a child he has a certain amount of time to get his homework done or he cannot go to a birthday party, the child may decide to go play outside instead of getting his assignment finished. The time for the birthday party arrives, and the parent tells the child he cannot go because he did not get his homework ready to be turned in the next day. The child may scream, "That's not fair! Other kids are going, and they were playing, too." The parent knows she is being totally fair.

The child was given the time needed to do his homework, and he had the knowledge of how to do the lesson. He simply chose not to, and the parent knows this. The parent also knows that some of the children who were out playing had finished their homework before they went outside. Some parents didn't really care whether or not their children did their homework at all. Other parents chose to let their children go to the birthday party as long as they finished their homework when they arrived home. The first parent did not use this technique because she knows her child would be too excited and would not settle down to finish his homework after the party. That is why she gave him the instructions to get his work done beforehand so he could go. Was the parent unfair when she said he could not go? The answer is no. Often this is exactly how we approach God.

Yeshua (Jesus) instructs us not to do something or to do something, and we choose to disobey. When negative consequences result, we scream, "That's not fair!" Picture the Lord standing in front of us, listening to our screams. When we're finished, He asks, "Didn't I tell you not to do that?" We answer, "Yes." He responds, "Didn't I tell you that consequences would be involved, the kind you wouldn't want?" We reply, "Yes." He replies, "Do you still think I am unfair?" We answer, "No." We realize He is much more than fair and deals with us with compassion that we do not deserve.

This was the situation Cain found himself in when God told Cain the consequences he would face after killing his brother Abel. Cain cried out, "My punishment [consequence] is greater than I can bear." God heard his cry and provided a way for Cain to deal with his situation.

Next, we will consider that which is truly not fair. Sometimes life stinks, it's hard, and it's not fair! Life is not fair when millions of children go home to millions of parents, and yet the children of a large number of parents will not come home due to kidnapping, an accident, or an illness that resulted in death. Life is not fair when a businessman runs a successful business and obeys all the rules, and his partner embezzles money. The embezzler bankrupts the businessman and leaves him to deal with all the consequences. Life is not fair when someone takes advantage of another and comes out on top. So, just what is the attitude of the Lord when life is truly not fair?

David was struck with this same dilemma. Please read Psalm 73. Focus in on verses 17 to 22, where God shows David three things—the consequences of his oppressors, the judgments in David's favor, and David's own bitterness—and David realized he was senseless and ignorant.

I had a woman in my life who for years brought me torment. She just loved to bring agony to my life. One day—and not to my credit—I secretly thought, "One of these days, you're going to get what's coming to you, and I'll be there to see it." Well, the Lord let me see that day, and I later wished I hadn't.

I was called to the home of this woman, where she had locked herself in her bathroom, refusing to let anyone in. Her children were concerned about her. When I arrived, I asked if I could come in, and she unlocked the door.

I walked in, and she was curled up in a ball and crying uncontrollably. In those moments, I realized that seeing her brought low like that did not erase all the hurtful years I had gone through with her. The experiences and the pain associated with them didn't go away. I thought seeing her suffering would make me feel better, but I didn't. I felt worse. I asked the Lord to forgive me for the bitterness I'd had for this woman for so many years.

The Lord showed me during that time that *I* was the senseless and ignorant one. By the time God was finished with me, I no longer wanted Him to set her in slippery places. I no longer wanted Him to cast her down in such agony. I no longer wanted to see her destroyed, faced with terror about what she would do next. Nor did I want Him to despise her form. As a matter of fact, I wanted and prayed for just the opposite for this woman.

I asked Him to heal her heart and her life, which was now in shreds and would be so for a long time to come. I also started asking how to be a blessing to this woman instead of a source of bitterness. As for the pain I suffered for years at the hands of this woman, God will heal it in His own time.

When life is truly not fair here, God will always judge in our favor. Knowing that our God is fair and will always be fair to us will allow us to move to the office of "Don't Deserve."


**\*For Small Groups**

Give all participants an opportunity to discuss their views of "Not Fair."

o   What are some additional ways Yeshua (Jesus) ministers to us concerning this topic?

o   Has anyone experienced a heart change from bitterness to blessing?

# Chapter 15

## The City Hall Office of "Don't Deserve"

In the previous chapter, we looked at two examples of how life may not be fair. During our visit in this office, the topic of "Don't Deserve" will be covered. The first item is something we can all appreciate.

Have you ever heard someone say, "I know she didn't do anything to deserve this gift. This present will make her happy, so I want to get it for her as a surprise. That's good enough for me"? That was how my step-dad, Bryan, treated my mother, Ann. He did that for years before she passed away. He bought her gifts consistently—not because he was celebrating her birthday, their anniversary, or the holidays, not because she won a Best Wife of the Year or Best Mother of the Year award. He bought her gifts because they brought her joy, and he had joy in giving them to her. This is a God trait. Yeshua (Jesus) gives us gifts every day, and He does it partly just because they bring smiles to our faces as we look up and say, "Thank you!" He does it to remind us that He is thinking of us.

Then there is another type of "Don't Deserve." This kind occurs when the punishment really doesn't fit the crime. The punishment is out of proportion. Tempers flare and retaliation is sought before any time is taken to assess the situation and come up with a reasonable course of action. The one on the receiving end will not come out of these situations without hurt feelings, to say the least. More often than we would like to admit, the outcomes for the one on the receiving end are painful on top of the hurt feelings. We have all heard the word "ultimatum"—using this word is not always a good course of action.

Laying down an ultimatum leads to misunderstandings, which in turn lead to even deeper hurts. With ultimatums, no opportunities exist for redemption to take place. We see this in action when someone yells out, "I'll never trust you again!"

The person on the receiving end hears the word "never." He interprets that statement to mean that only one of two choices can be made: either stay in a relationship with no chance or no way to redeem himself or leave. He chooses to leave. Meanwhile, the person who screamed that sentence out has calmed down and is ready to face the situation. But now it may be too late. The person screamed at has left. This is very detrimental, often to both parties, but usually the one who leaves is hurt more.

This way of handling a situation is not a God trait. God always leaves room for redemption if the person is willing to do what it takes to avoid repeating the hurtful behavior. This option is not presented as one of the choices in an ultimatum. Now, we're left with pain. One often hears statements like "She didn't deserve to be treated that way. You were too hard on her, and now she's gone." Deep hurt leads to bad choices, and we're off.

Let's consider a couple of methods to solve this kind of problem. One plan is to assess the state of things before ultimatums are laid down and look for a discipline to match the transgression. We should be able to see a light at the end of the tunnel—and not that of an oncoming train! Young children are given a time-out. Older children lose certain privileges for a time. Teens may not be allowed to drive or be with friends for a while. In each of these cases, discipline has a time frame, and hope exists at the end that the persons involved can work out better alternatives to their behavior. Some parents come up with two or three consequences and involve the children in choosing their own punishment.

This is all well and good before ultimatums, but what happens when things have gotten out of hand, and the situation has blown up?

Sometimes people do leave, and reconciling is not an option. But one thing we do know is that God has a direction in mind, and He will ultimately guide the outcome. Read Proverbs 16:9. This proverb states that our minds (the mind of man) come up with plans, but the Lord directs our steps. When someone leaves, we're faced with a fork in the road. We may cross paths again and reconcile at a different time down the road. We may not reconcile until the resurrection. We may never reconcile. Whatever the outcome, God does and will direct our steps. We just need to accept Him and follow His direction for our lives and the lives of those we love. He also hears our prayers for those we miss while they are away from us.

Next, we're going to look at the thoughts and feelings that assert someone doesn't deserve forgiveness because someone is or was so bad.

Has anyone heard the phrases "She (or he) doesn't deserve to be forgiven!" or "They don't deserve to be forgiven! I hope they rot! If they were standing in the middle of the street and a truck hit them, I wouldn't cross the street or lift a finger to help them! I hope they suffer forever!" People with this attitude have several unhealed areas in their lives. Anger of this magnitude will be explored further in the chapter ahead. For now, we need to have a starting place.

When someone states that another person doesn't deserve to be forgiven, that statement is correct. When we sin, we do not warrant forgiveness. When others sin against us, they do not have the right to be forgiven. Sin hurts every time to different degrees—period—and no one deserves to be forgiven of sins. We do not work toward forgiving people because they deserve it. We work toward forgiving people because they *don't* deserve it! We don't work toward accepting forgiveness for our sins from Yeshua (Jesus) because we deserve to be forgiven but because we don't. Yeshua (Jesus) freely offers and grants us forgiveness so that we can become a conduit of His forgiveness toward others as well. This will be the place to begin.

At the very top of a sheet of paper, write "Yeshua (Jesus)." Divide the paper in half, and write on the top of one half "Yeshua (Jesus) has forgiven me for:" and fill in a list of sins you have committed. Don't leave any out. On the other side of the paper, write "Yeshua (Jesus) has forgiven you for:" and fill in the list of sins that have been committed against you by someone specific. Don't leave any out. Now we're going to examine a piece of the puzzle in not forgiving someone.

Yeshua (Jesus) is not going to be upset if you and I don't forgive someone when we do not have the information or tools necessary to achieve that goal. He will be upset when we do not offer His forgiveness toward the people who have sinned against us but instead keep His forgiveness for ourselves alone. His death and resurrection paid the price for all who receive Him. Read Hebrews 7:25–27, focusing on verse 27.

Once you complete the exercise above, you have begun to fulfill the requirement in Matthew 6:14–15 by releasing the forgiveness of Yeshua (Jesus) into the lives of people who have sinned against you until you can finish the course. Remember prayer. We can ask God to forgive those who have sinned against us, and we're totally within His will to do so. Read 2 Peter 3:9. Whenever we are dealing with sins causing a hornet's nest of pain in our lives—whether they are sins we have committed or sins others have committed against us—we have Yeshua (Jesus) as our remedy.

He doesn't stop at forgiveness. He also provides instructions on how to deal with sins so that they do not continue to plague us. Before we get to those instructions, let's take a look at the next office, "Too Angry."

**\*For Small Groups**

Give everyone an opportunity to discuss the attitude concerning people not deserving to be forgiven.

o   What are some ideas to help us overcome this attitude?

o   How easy is the exercise with the piece of paper to use to see how to receive and give the forgiveness of Yeshua (Jesus)?

# Chapter 16

## The City Hall Office of "Too Angry"

The office of "Too Angry" has several departments. The departments are as follows: Anger toward Self, Anger toward Others, Anger of Others Directed at Us, Anger of Others Directed at Themselves, and Anger against God.

An understanding of anger and its causes will be helpful here. Anger is defined as extreme displeasure toward someone or several persons, an event, or something. Wrathfulness, violent hostility, detestability, hatred, and lividness are a few other descriptions of anger. Some causes of anger are linked to sin.

Sins we have committed but not taken responsibility for cause anger. Sins committed against us to the point where we feel we don't deserve to be treated well can cause us to turn anger toward ourselves. Not being treated fairly or with respect causes anger. Some causes of anger are not linked to sin. One such source of anger occurs when we defend someone who is helpless, such as a child or an animal. They cannot defend themselves against an attack, so we step in. Before we begin to cover the topic of anger toward self and others, we are going to lay some groundwork.

If we cannot see ourselves forgiving someone at this time, can we at least see that God has forgiven those who sinned against us through the death of His Son? Yeshua (Jesus) died once for all who receive Him as Lord and Savior. Read Romans 6:10. Can we also picture areas of our life where His Spirit is living inside us?

How would we recognize His Spirit as living in us? Have we ever shown kindness to someone or to an animal? Have we ever spoken a kind word to someone? Have we ever felt compassion for another? Have we ever shown or given encouragement to another? Support can come through a hug or a simple handshake. Have we ever felt agape love from another or given agape love to another? Read 1 John 4:7. We know God is agape love. When we express His love, we know we are of Him and we are born of Him. We know during the times we show His agape love in word and deed that He is living in us.

We can all recollect times where we have given and received kindness. The next question, then, is, can we conceive of the idea that Yeshua (Jesus) through His Spirit has the ability to live in us more fully? Read Galatians 2:20. With the knowledge that Yeshua (Jesus) lives in us, the next piece of groundwork is ready to be put in place.

The work we are going to do right now is pray a very specific prayer: Lord Yeshua (Jesus), we come before You and ask You to fill us with Your Holy Spirit. We ask You to take away and remove our bitterness, wrath, anger, clamor, and malice that we have held in our hearts toward anyone. We ask You to fill our hearts with Yourself, Your heart, and Your characteristics of kindness, compassion, forgiveness, humility, gentleness, patience, and love for the persons who have hurt us. In the name of Yeshua (Jesus), amen.

The groundwork of prayer is very important, because without the Spirit of Yeshua (Jesus), forgiveness will elude us. Knowing the characteristics of Yeshua (Jesus) is extremely significant so that we can recognize when He's living through us and when He isn't. He will honor this prayer and come and live in us. Read Galatians 2:20 and Philippians 4:13.

Yeshua (Jesus) did not go to the cross out of a heart of bitterness, wrath, anger, clamor, slander, malice, condemnation, or judgment against us. He went to the cross with a heart full of kindness, a tender heart, a forgiving heart, a heart full of compassion, and a heart full of His agape love for us. It is the kindness of the Lord that leads us to repentance. When we are instructed to lay aside bitterness, wrath, anger, clamor, condemnation, and judgment against another, we are at the same time asked to pick up the heart and characteristics of Yeshua (Jesus). No bitterness can exist in our hearts toward ourselves or others with the agape love and forgiveness of Yeshua (Jesus). Bitterness and forgiveness are opposites. They cannot coexist. They will separate just like oil and water.

We are now going to put a second piece of groundwork in place. We have concepts of what we are to put away and what we are to pick up, but what do they look like in reality that goes beyond something vague, like the word "bitterness"? Bitterness is like being in a severe snowstorm with such high winds that the snow stings and cuts our skin. Bitterness of the heart is anguish taken to an extreme level and causes acute pain in our lives or the lives of others.

So, what does wrath look like?

Wrath is similar to a volatile, violent eruption of a volcano, where not all come out alive—and those who do survive do not come through without scars.

Anger was described earlier in the chapter. What about clamor?

Clamor is similar to ultimatums, where demands or complaints never come to an end. We see this in action in Proverbs 21:19, which states that it is better to live in a desert than with a contentious woman.

What about slander?

Slander means saying untrue statements that cause harm to another's well-being or cause injury to their reputation. This is found as one of the Ten Commandments—thou shall not bear false witness against your neighbor—in the book of Exodus.

Next is malice, which is the desire to see others suffer without just cause. There would be no just cause to for someone to poke someone else's eye out just because he or she was waiting to check out at a grocery store. Malice is hatred in the heart to hurt people intentionally using harmful words and actions.

We have looked at a few characteristics, what they resemble, and what we are to turn away from. Now let us look at characteristics we are to turn to. We will begin with kindness.

Kindness can begin with a kind word, a word of encouragement, or a simple gesture, like a hug. Kindness can be compared to an animal shelter or animal rescue where animals are taken care of rather than being treated cruelly or neglected. Kindness can also be a generous gesture, such as paying for a dinner for someone else or opening a door.

What does compassion look like?

Compassion could be compared to sharing the suffering experience of another. We see this in action when Yeshua (Jesus) wept with Mary before He raised Lazarus from the dead. We also see in

Romans 12:15 the instruction to rejoice with those who rejoice and weep with those who weep.

What does humility look like?

Humility is evident in people who are on their knees or have their faces on the ground, showing submission to God. Yeshua (Jesus) in the garden of Gethsemane submitting to the will of His Father, willingly accepting what was soon to become agony for Him, is what humility looks like.

What does gentleness resemble?

Gentleness is like a cool, refreshing breeze. It's not stale, as in no breeze at all, nor is it fierce like a windstorm. Most everyone has been outside on a hot day when a breeze came along to gently cool the air.

What is patience equivalent to?

When we consider patience, think of someone taking care of another person with a long-term illness and seeing to that person's needs with a positive and good attitude toward both the person and the situation.

A few words will not be defined so that you can discover their meanings for yourself. This will help grow your relationship in the Lord.

Now, let's put a third piece of groundwork in place. This piece defines what forgiveness *is not*. Forgiveness is not condoning the sin or sins that took place or that are taking place. Forgiveness is not agreeing that the sins that took place or are taking place are okay—they are not. The sins from the fall of creation were just as wrong then as they are today. Sins will be just as wrong in the future by His definition. Yeshua (Jesus) doesn't agree with or approve of committing sin.

In two places in the New Testament, Yeshua (Jesus) spoke to the persons involved and instructed them to go and not sin again. He instructed one man to go and not sin again lest something worse should befall him. Yeshua (Jesus) was trying to explain that something worse in the life of the man would happen to him or affect his life that he would not want, so He told the man not to sin again. Yeshua (Jesus) did not put His stamp of approval on sin nor does He today—nor will He in the future. Forgiveness does not mean escaping the consequences of sin.

If someone gambles a few thousand dollars away, he or she may be forgiven for gambling the money away but does not receive the gambled money back. With sin come effects. We can read from Genesis to Revelation, and we will see that consequences do not go away. The story of David and Bathsheba illustrates this principle. Forgiveness was made available for both of them through the sacrificial system in place at that time; however, God told David that as part of the issues he would face, the sword would never part from his house again. Forgiveness is not going to erase or change all the pain suffered.

If someone steals a beloved pet out of someone else's yard, the person may forgive the thief, but the loss of the pet will still be felt—and the sorrow with it. The tears cried existed. Tears cried today are going to fall—that won't change. The pain was or is real and does not change with forgiveness.

Forgiveness is not being coerced, threatened, or accused of not being forgiving. When we look at forgiveness as a way to manipulate being forgiven via accusations or threats, we have missed the whole point of forgiveness and what it really is. We are now going to learn what forgiveness is and how to apply it.

Forgiveness is seeing the pain sin inflicts on the lives of others and then letting go of any ill feelings connected to the pain and sins, letting God be judge of the final consequences. Knowing that Yeshua (Jesus) was beaten, spit on, reviled, and hung on a cross is painful for us, realizing He went through all that for us in order to deal with our sins. We need to recognize that when we sin against others or others sin against us, real pain is delivered to the lives of everyone involved.

Every single person pays a price for sins against them at their expense. Each one of us pays a price for people who sin against us at our expense. When we sin against ourselves, we pay a price. Acknowledgment of pain and suffering must be brought to the table in forgiveness.

When we see Yeshua (Jesus) and His suffering, we fall on our knees and weep over what our sins cost Him and His life for us. We also need to recognize that sin against one another causes suffering. As we become aware of the anguish to ourselves and others, we need to own up to specifics and to the cost—and then address forgiveness.

Seven steps are involved for total forgiveness to take place. Step one is naming the person or persons involved. When people cannot be named, such as an attacker, we can simply name an attacker "stranger."
Step two is identifying the sins with specific names. The reason we need the names of the sins is to obtain a clear understanding of what we are forgiving a person for. Here's an example: I forgive _____ (the person has been named) for stealing my watch (the sin identified). If a watch has

been stolen, then we may need to protect ourselves and the person involved from the temptation that caused them to sin in the first place. We could just put our watches away while that person is in the house. Part of the prayer of Yeshua (Jesus) asks for us not to lead us into temptation. Likewise, we are not to lead others into temptation either when it's in our power to do so.

The third step necessary in forgiveness is to be allowed to communicate without judgment or condemnation when sinned against. Whether sins were or are against us or against others, we all need to voice how the sins affected our lives and attitudes. Being articulate about the effects of sin is a statement of truth.

Step four is where we go from here. We now ask for the blood of Yeshua (Jesus) through His Holy Spirit of compassion, mercy, and forgiveness of the person or persons involved to come in and cover the sins with His agape love and His blood.

Step five is making the transition from unhealthy feelings to healthy feelings by absorbing and applying the characteristics of Yeshua (Jesus) to the person(s) and sin(s) involved.

The sixth step is to speak and keep our new proclamation concerning the person(s) and sin(s) we are dealing with. The seventh step is allowing God to deal with the final outcome.

The following chapters represent four exercises. The applications to practice are similar, yet each deals with a unique situation. Let's begin with ourselves.


**\*For Small Groups** Give everyone an opportunity to discuss the seven steps to forgiveness.

# Chapter 17

## Anger toward Self and Others

We will begin by being truthful and honest with what God's Word says about us. As we progress, we will continue to follow His lead.

Read 1 John 1:8–10. These verses tell us that when we say we have no sin, we are deceiving ourselves, we make God a liar, and His truth about us is not in us. He doesn't leave us without hope, and this is where we continue to follow His lead. In verse 9, He states that if we confess our sins (the choice is ours), He is faithful, and it's His right to forgive and cleanse us from all unrighteousness. When Yeshua (Jesus) cleanses us from unrighteousness, He also imparts righteousness to us as part of our cleansing.

Think about falling in the mud and taking a bath to clean up. After the shower, there is no more mud. If mud is the equivalent of unrighteousness, then lack of mud is the equivalent of righteousness. Now we get a clearer picture of how God sees humankind, including us, with regard to cleansing.

This is the starting place to believe (embrace new thoughts about ourselves and others, act in right ways, and embrace good feelings about ourselves and others). When we do not confess our sins, anger and bitterness toward ourselves take up residency within our minds. There is a truth here. Until we embrace and experience for ourselves the agape love and forgiveness of Yeshua (Jesus), we will not be able to successfully grant forgiveness from our hearts to someone else.

If I were to ask each person around me to give me a quarter, they probably could. If I asked each person in my presence to give me $100,000, most of them won't have it. Once we know and own in our hearts, minds, and spirits that our sins are covered by the blood of Yeshua (Jesus) out of His agape love and compassion for us, we can then bring Him to the people who have sinned against us.

Picture yourself in front of someone you seriously sinned against. The person you envision can include yourself.

If you find yourself dealing with various numbers of people, think of only one person at a time. We are not going to make allowances to get crushed in spirit to the point of defeat by becoming overwhelmed. If we discover that too many people or number of sins are being seen all at once, then write one name in big bold letters on a piece of paper and place that name in front of you. This will keep your attention pinpointed. Deal with one sin at a time.

We need to overcome one situation with one person at a time, otherwise we risk feeling beaten down too much and will give up before we are victorious.

What is required of us to win a victory? If we look to any battle that is won, we recognize that we are not alone. No one is alone when dealing with the whole sin issue, whether we are talking of our sins or the sins of others. Another aspect of winning a battle is that we have someone who is in it with us—Yeshua (Jesus). Additional supports can be at least two or three trustworthy, intimate friends who are a source of encouragement.

Strategies are in place to assist in winning a war. By focusing on one person and one sin at a time, we will win the battle.

Next, we will consider not providing an escape concerning the people we sinned against. Do not allow yourself to get away with saying, "I can't handle seeing you this way because of what I did or because of me." At the time the sin was committed, difficulty of bringing pain into the life of someone you sinned against was not enough to prevent it or to stop yourself.

When thinking of the person to be dealt with, there may not have been a problem blaming or accusing him or her in order to justify yourself for your actions and words. Although perhaps a sorrowful experience, we could witness a small portion of the anguish we have brought to someone that the person has subsequently had to live with, experience, and work through. We are not going to give ourselves an out. No outs, no excuses, no justification on our part.

We are after the plain truth about specific sins that we have committed against ourselves or others. We are not going to provide a key to give us an out by saying, "It's okay; don't cry." This is *sin* we're talking about. It's not supposed to feel comfortable. As with any successful battle, there are prizes at the end of the war.

The battle we're involved in involves making a transition from unforgiveness to receiving forgiveness for ourselves and others through the blood of Yeshua (Jesus). We will win the battle with perseverance. Many weapons are made of steel. But one of our weapons is the Word of the Lord, as pure as silver tried in a furnace seven times—purified.

Imagine that we have two twenty-five-cent coins in our pockets. One of the coins is to remind us that we are forgiven. This exercise involves dealing with anger toward ourselves. For some of us, a more direct approach is needed in order to hear our own confession. We are going to confess our sin(s) without condemnation or judgment against ourselves, saying something like, "When the sin of _____ was committed (sin identified), a lot of pain was brought into my life. Because of my sins against you, a lot of pain was also brought into your life. Both of our lives were deeply affected on several levels. There was a time when I felt bitterness and anger toward myself for the sins I committed. I have asked (am asking) the Lord through His blood, compassion, mercy, forgiveness, and His agape love for me to come and cover the sin(s) involved. I'll not feel bitter about those incidents any longer. I have also asked the Lord to live inside me with His heart. He answered my prayer, and I have Yeshua (Jesus) living within me. I have the heart of Yeshua (Jesus) toward myself and the sins involved, replacing the bitterness and anger I held against myself for so long. I have His characteristics of forgiveness, compassion, and kindness toward myself. I'll do what I can to make a positive difference in your life from now on. I am sorry."

We need to own His agape love for ourselves. Our ability to receive forgiveness or give forgiveness to another person does not rest on ourselves alone, but we can be and are successful with Yeshua (Jesus) every time. Our confession is not to be used as a way to dishonor someone we have sinned against by using God as an out.

When we sin against other people, they may need to express their own emotions. We do not begin to deal with our own obligations until we accept accountability for our words, choices, and actions toward ourselves and others. When we take on liability for someone else, we are not holding ourselves responsible correctly. God did not hold Eve at fault for the circumstances Adam faced. He also did not hold Adam accountable for the conditions Eve faced. Neither should we. We are not responsible for the pain of others that has been brought to our lives through their sins committed against us, but we are responsible for our own healing of that pain.

Our next subject will be anger against others. When we hold on to the feelings of anger and bitterness toward another, the cause is that someone has sinned grievously against us. When we do not acknowledge sins committed against us, our unhealthy emotions become domiciled within our minds toward others. The following exercise is designed to bring the forgiveness of Yeshua (Jesus) to someone or several who have sinned against us.

Begin by picturing someone who has sinned against you severely. Again, if there are several people, see only one person in front of you at a time. Do not get overwhelmed with a vision of more than one person. If you find yourself going off track and seeing others, write one name in big, bold letters on a piece of paper and place that name in front of you. This will keep your focus. This next area is not to be overcome with sins against you. Deal with one sin at a time. Keep your attention on one person with one sin involved. When there are many sins, make a list of them, placing the most difficult ones at the top. Begin by going down the list, marking off one at a time as you are able.

The next thing to consider is not to provide an escape for the person who sinned against you. Do not let them get away with saying something like, "I can't stand to see the pain you are experiencing because of what I brought into your life." The person who sinned against you did not have enough of a problem bringing pain into your life initially to prevent him or her from doing so.

The person you are dealing with may not have had a problem blaming or accusing you in order to justify themselves for their actions and words. He or she can see a small portion of the sorrow you have had to live with, dealt with in reality, and labored with to get to a good place.

The next thing we should do when dealing with those who have hurt us is to not allow people to absolve themselves in order to rationalize their hurtful actions toward us. It is human nature to try to justify our actions to ourselves, but this is no excuse for hurting those around us. We are after truth, clearly naming sins committed against us. We are not going to give him or her an out. We are not going to provide anyone with a key that says, "Oh, it's okay; don't cry." Each of us is going to achieve the goal of being a forgiving person.

As individuals, receiving and giving forgiveness makes every pilgrimage separate from anyone else. Each of us is dealing with different people and our personal relationships with them. Two people may actually be dealing with the same person; however, each person involved has his or her own separate story due to differing experiences and perceptions. At the same time, we are not on separate journeys, because Yeshua (Jesus) is incorporated with us in our travels. He is permanently involved with us. In agreement and in cooperation with God, all things are possible.

In the following exercise, picture someone who sinned against you. With the person's likeness in front of you, say something like, "When the sin of _____ was committed (sin identified), I felt a lot of pain. My life was deeply affected and in chaos in several areas as a result. There was a time when I felt bitterness and anger toward you and the sins committed. I have asked (am asking) the Lord through His blood, compassion, mercy, forgiveness, and His agape love for you to come and cover the sin(s) committed against me at that time. I no longer have feelings of bitterness about those incidents. I have also asked the Lord to live inside of me with His heart. He answered my prayer, and I have the heart of Yeshua (Jesus) living within me. I have His character of forgiveness, compassion, and kindness toward you."

You may need to repeat this exercise multiple times when several different people are included or when a specific sin is repeated over and over. Remember to handle one person and one sin at a time.

Repeat the above exercise as many times as needed. Earlier, we mentioned two twenty-five-cent coins, one of which was to remind us that we are forgiven. The remaining quarter is for us to give to someone who Yeshua (Jesus) and we have forgiven, as a reminder to them.

When we complete the above exercise, we have fulfilled the requirements given in Matthew 6:14–15 forgiving someone from our heart. This exercise works every time without fail. The agape love of Yeshua (Jesus) never fails. Keep your focus on being forgiven and being a forgiving person.

When bitterness has had a long-term foothold, sometimes we need a little extra help letting go of harmful feelings. We will now take a little detour.

**\*For Small Groups**

Give everyone an opportunity to discuss the challenge to be truthful and honest about ourselves according to the Word of God.

o   Is forgiving someone easier after we have experienced the forgiveness of Yeshua (Jesus) for ourselves?

o   Discuss no outs, no excuses.

o   Who besides Yeshua (Jesus) are companions one can call on for support? Name two or three.

o   What are some additional strategies that could assist us in not being overwhelmed by our own sins or the sins of others against us?

o   Were the exercises difficult?

o   Can you see yourself carrying two quarters? Can you see yourself keeping one to remind yourself that you are forgiven, loved, valued, and esteemed with compassion from Yeshua (Jesus) and giving the other away to someone who sinned against you to let them know they are forgiven, loved, valued, and esteemed with compassion from Yeshua (Jesus)?

\*\*\*

And now for the detour.

Bitterness that is deeply ingrained in our lives must be dealt with in a unique way. When bitterness has been a large part of our lives for months or even years, it can develop into a stronghold. When this occurs, additional aid is needed to embrace healthy emotions once again.

Read Ephesians 4:31–32. Let all of it—the complete package of bitterness, wrath, unhealthy anger, clamor, slander, and malice—be put away from you. Be tenderhearted, forgiving each other just as God in Messiah (Christ) has also forgiven you. These two verses are tied together.

The latter part of the verse is just as God in Messiah (Christ) has also forgiven (past tense) you. What has He forgiven? All the bitterness, wrath, unhealthy anger, clamor, slander, and malice we have held in our hearts toward ourselves and others. Yeshua (Jesus) knew in advance that certain sins would provoke these negative emotions, and for a time He is okay that we feel them. But there comes a time to put them away and put on His heart of kindness, compassion, mercy, and forgiveness.

We are not to deposit sins of bitterness, wrath, unhealthy anger, and so on into the lives of others. This leads to the question of how to deal with our anger when we are feeling rage.

We are not to pretend, ignore, or sweep under the rug our feelings of indignation when we feel them. We are to acknowledge their existence as our valid feelings. We are not to spew a sewage hose of anger all over another person. We are to have the heart of Yeshua (Jesus) toward the persons we are feeling angry with before we come together with them. We recognize that Yeshua (Jesus) seeks to heal through our being kindhearted to one another.

In James 1:20, we recognize that the wrath of humankind does not accomplish the righteousness of God. If the anger we are feeling is destructive and likely to deposit rage or accusation into the life of another, the time has not yet arrived to come together. When this occurs, we need to back off for a time. This is a time to recognize any unhealthy anger we must deal with.

We are not to let the sun go down on our wrath, but this does not mean we puke hurtful anger all over someone with all kinds of negative words or actions before the sun sets. It does not mean we are always going to be over feeling angry before the sun sets, either—nor are we expected to be. If an arm gets broken in the morning, it probably won't be healed by nightfall. When great hurts occur, they won't be healed by the time the sun sets. Major hurts need time to heal, just like any severe injury. What the Word is talking about is for us to begin to seek healing for our anger issue before the sun sets. We may need to get physical but not harmful.

When dealing with unhealthy anger, we may need to take a walk, jog, split some wood, scream into a pillow, or choke a fence post. Physical activity such as hitting a few baseballs or playing a round of tennis may be just what is needed to burn off some of the hot flames of anger. Before the sun goes down, we are on our knees confessing harmful anger, receiving the blood covering and forgiveness of Yeshua (Jesus) over our cruel wrath.

We're confessing and pleading the love of Yeshua (Jesus) to cover the sins and the situations involved that provoked the feeling of rage and allowed it to surface so that we can lay the harmful emotions aside. We begin to seek healing before the sun goes down. Who knows? We just may be healed before bedtime.

If we're not quite ready to lay aside our anger, the time has come to learn about being transferred. Before we begin, here is a list items you may need:

- Two clear sandwich bags

- A pen or pencil
- A black marker
- One smaller clear bag that will fit inside one of the sandwich bags
- Several white cotton balls, poms, or Styrofoam balls and several black cotton balls, poms, or Styrofoam balls, sized to fit inside the sandwich bags
- Paper to write on
- Tape or self-adhesive labels

Gathering these items together is not necessary to complete the book; however, they can be helpful because people learn in different ways. Some people can simply read and comprehend a story and continue to move on through while others need to physically see what is done in order to understand a concept.

For example, I have sometimes had trouble understanding how to sew a specific pattern together. I could not grasp what the instructions were trying to convey until I sought help and watched someone else assemble the pieces. Once I saw how the pieces came together, I could go home and complete the item I was sewing.

Another group of people need hands-on learning. A person can read up on how to drive a car but may not have the full understanding until the car is driven. At that point, the person has more knowledge about how and why the vehicle operates as it does.

In this section of the book, all three methods will be used. Some will hear and understand God's Word. Some will see how God's Word works. Others will perform the actions of God's Word (hands on) to comprehend His message. Use whatever method works for you to acquire the most benefit.

For the purposes of this book, I will be using white and black cotton balls. We will begin in the book of Colossians. In the opening verses, Paul introduces himself and explains whom he is writing to. He offers thanks to God. He makes us understand that he is praying and for whom. He puts into plain language the reasons he prays. On your own, read Colossians 1:1–8. Then, beginning with verse 9, read and personalize the prayer from Colossians 1:9–14. You can end the prayer in the name of Yeshua (Jesus), amen.

Now, take the two clear sandwich bags. On one bag, write with a marker "DoD," representing "Domain of Darkness." On the other bag, write with a marker "KoS," to represent "Kingdom of Son" (Son of God).

Next, on a small piece of paper or self-adhesive label, write with a pen Colossians 1:13(a): "For He delivered us from the domain of darkness." Tape or stick this label to the smaller bag that will be placed inside the larger DoD and KoS bags. Place a white cotton ball inside the smaller bag. Take this little bag and place it inside the DoD bag just for a moment.

Next, write on a small piece of paper or label Colossians 1:13(b): "And transferred us to the kingdom of His beloved Son." Tape or stick this label on the outside of the KoS bag.

Next, take the smaller bag out of the DoD bag. Take the white cotton ball out of the smaller bag and place it inside the KoS bag.

Next, take the smaller bag, now empty, and put it back inside the DoD bag.

The above instructions were given because God's Word is going to show us a few things. One is that God made a transfer. He transferred us from the domain of darkness to the kingdom of His beloved Son. Nothing you or I could do using our own strength could get out of the domain of darkness. God made our transfer. Notice that our transfer is complete. Pay attention to the difference between the two kingdoms. The kingdom of darkness is different than the kingdom of light.

The kingdom of darkness is bound up in bitterness, wrath, unhealthy anger, and so on. The kingdom of light consists of kindness, compassion, forgiveness of Yeshua (Jesus), and so on. Since all have sinned, all have at one time or another been in the DoD. But God, in His agape love for us, didn't leave us there. He transferred us. Look at the two baggies. The smaller bag inside the DoD bag is now empty. The KoS bag is not empty. Make a joyful noise. The bag that isn't empty is the KoS (kingdom of God's Son), which represents where every believer in Yeshua (Jesus) resides. Continuing on, it is written in Colossians 1:14 that we have redemption and forgiveness of sins.

Now, take another label and write Colossians 1:14. "in whom we have redemption, the forgiveness of sins." and stick this verse on the outside of the KoS bag. Next, take two white cotton balls and put them inside the KoS bag, where you reside. One cotton ball represents redemption, and the other represents forgiveness. Read Colossians 3:8. Put them all aside—unhealthy anger, wrath, malice, slander, and abusive speech. Now, take another label and write Colossians 3:8. "But now you also, put them all aside: anger, wrath, malice, slander, and abusive speech from your mouth." and then stick this label on the DoD bag.

Take five black cotton balls and put them inside the DoD bag to represent Colossians 3:8. Read Colossians 3:12–14. Take eleven white cotton balls and place them inside the KoS baggie. These cotton balls represent that we are chosen of God, we are holy, and we are His beloved. In addition, we have the compassion, kindness, humility, gentleness, patience, bearing, forgiveness, and agape love of Yeshua (Jesus). Take another label, write Colossians 3:12–14. "And so, as those who have been chosen of God, holy and beloved, put on a heart of compassion, kindness, humility, gentleness and patience: bearing with one another, and forgiving each other, whoever has a complaint against anyone; just as the Lord forgave you, so also should you. And beyond all these things put on love, which is the perfect bond of unity." and stick it on the KoS bag. Notice that we are on the inside of the bag while the verses are on the outside of the bag surrounding us. This is a picture of what we look like *in* Messiah (Christ).

Romans 8:1 tells us that there is therefore now no condemnation for those *in* Messiah (Christ) Yeshua (Jesus). Look at the KoS bag, and read the labels. As we study the verses, we will see there are no black balls in the KoS bag. Yeshua (Jesus) only has His compassion, kindness, humility, gentleness, patience, bearing, forgiveness, and agape love for us. First John 1:5 tells us that God is light, and in Him there is no darkness at all. No matter how many times we examine the KoS bag, a black ball will never be found. Colossians 3:12–14 is also a picture of what the Holy Spirit of Yeshua (Jesus) surrounding us looks like. We're going to get an even larger picture.

The more we embrace the characteristics of Yeshua (Jesus) toward us and own them for ourselves, the more we are placed in a position for God to reveal a mystery. The mystery He wants us to see is Messiah (Christ) living in us and through us, which makes us the hope of His glory. Yeshua (Jesus) living in us empowers us to forgive, bringing His forgiveness to people who need Him. As we allow Yeshua (Jesus) through His Holy Spirit to live through us, we have His compassion, kindness, humility, gentleness, patience, bearing, forgiveness, and agape love for those who sinned against us.

Give yourself a high five. From here, we will begin to go to warmer temperatures yet by conquering the five Ts.

## *For Small Groups

Give everyone an opportunity to discuss the concepts of the DoD and KoS bags.

o   What are some thoughts about putting all bitterness, wrath, anger, clamor, slander, and malice away—no longer entertaining those attitudes toward ourselves or others? What are some healthy outlets for anger?

o   By which method do you personally receive the most benefit when learning a new concept— read and comprehend, see and understand, or hands on?

Can you remember times in your life before you were delivered to the kingdom of God's Son?

o How was life different when you realized you were transferred to the kingdom of God's Son?

o Is the meaning of you *in* Messiah (Christ) Yeshua (Jesus) easy to understand?

o Is the idea of Messiah (Christ) in you evident?

o Are there characteristic traits of Yeshua (Jesus) that you would like to improve on?

o What are some methods we could use to hold on to and put into practice the compassion, kindness, humility, gentleness, patience, bearing, forgiveness, and agape love of Yeshua (Jesus) for us and others?

***

Ready for warmer weather? Our next study will help us return to warmer temperatures.

The five Ts are as follows: tribulation, temptation, troubles, tests, and trials. Not only will we see the differences but we will also be victorious in each of these areas. Begin by recognizing those pesky spirits not from the Lord known as bitterness, wrath, unhealthy anger, clamor, and malice. Once we understand that these feelings are not from Yeshua (Jesus), we also understand their source, which leads us to tribulation. Tribulation is Satan trying to maintain a foothold of bitterness and other unhealthy emotions by reminding us through memories.

Memories come in two forms: we are either reminded of the losses and pain we suffered, or we remember losses and pain we have caused others.

Using recollection, Satan tries to move us to temptation, where we are enticed to pick up again the feelings of bitterness, wrath, unhealthy anger, clamor, and malice. He tries this technique by being subtle, usually in the form of questions.

The questions he may ask are, "Don't you remember the pain you suffered at their hands? Have you forgotten the misery they inflicted on you? Aren't you feeling just a little angry with them right now?" When he finds that recalling past sins committed against us doesn't work, he will use our past against us with the use of different questions, such as, "Don't you remember the agony that person suffered at your hands? Have you forgotten the misery you inflicted on them? Aren't you feeling just a little angry with yourself right now?" Keep in mind that he is suggesting unhealthy anger. Satan's goal is to cause us trouble and create enough distress to make our commitment to forgiveness difficult.

But here is where we win the victory. By recognizing those troublesome spirits, we have the knowledge of being put to a test. Here's how to pass the test and defeat Satan and his influence. When any of the unhealthy spirits such as bitterness or unhealthy anger try to draw us back into those negative feelings, we say something like, "No, I refuse to feel bitter about those incidents any longer. I have the heart of Yeshua (Jesus) living within me. I have His character of forgiveness, compassion, and kindness toward myself and those persons involved." Speaking a proclamation of where we stand today does not mean the pain we went through will never be felt again, and that's okay.

We may cry six months from now. We may cry ten years from now, especially with severe losses, but we do not have to embrace bitterness or condemnation along with the tears. Our tears can just be acknowledged, felt, and released. What it does mean is that we are choosing the forgiveness of Yeshua (Jesus) to cover painful experiences and let Him dry our tears in His time. By the time we have reached this point, we have passed the test. Not only did we pass but we know how to be victorious every time from this point on.

To maintain victory, we may need to remind ourselves of our new choices. For some, bitterness has held a strong foothold in their lives for an expanded length of time. Those feelings can be combated by renewing our minds to our new choices.

To maintain our triumph, we may need to carry a couple of cards to read on a regular basis until we have fully integrated those beliefs as ours. Our cards will serve as a reminder to us. The first card can read something like, "I know I asked the Lord through His blood, compassion, mercy, forgiveness, and His agape love for myself (you) to come and cover the sin(s) involved that were committed at that time. I know He has answered this prayer for me, because His word says all sins shall be forgiven the sons of men save one."

The second card may read something like, "I no longer feel bitter about those incidents. I have the heart of Yeshua (Jesus) living within me. I have His character of forgiveness, compassion, and kindness toward myself or you, one of the persons who hurt me." Renewing our minds will yield great benefits as we continue to grow in Yeshua (Jesus).

Sometimes we may need a tangible item to carry with us as well as the written words on our cards. Several people choose to wear a ring or necklace as an object they can touch when their cards are not handy. Others carry a small item in their pocket, like a marble, a stone, or a couple of quarters. Some of us have T-shirts printed up with words written on them. Find whatever works for you when you need more than a card or two.

Yeshua (Jesus) forgives us. He teaches us how to forgive others, and we reap the rewards of being forgiving. The more we exercise His agape love, kindness, and compassion toward ourselves and others, the more we are rewarded by being happier. We gain by being the person Yeshua (Jesus) wants us to become. Becoming the person Yeshua (Jesus) wants us to become places us in position to be His disciples by bringing Him to humankind.

A trial is like being placed in court. When we stand with conviction and say that we value Yeshua (Jesus) and His character in our hearts, minds, and spirits over and above those of Satan, we pass the trial. Court is dismissed. We are found blameless. Not only are we embracing His characteristics, we're students of what they are and how to apply them to our lives and the lives of others. Our minds can change from concentrating on the negative feelings to positive feelings and how to grow in them. The qualities of Yeshua (Jesus) that we grow in are part of the plunder we win at the end of a war. More treasure is to be had, and it involves losing unhealthy fear.

Fear on a healthy level can warn us by keeping us safe, like inciting us not to walk too close to the edge of a ledge from which we could suffer a dangerous fall. There is a debilitating fear of having our sins found out by others and of what others would think. This mind-set creates a protective mechanism where we are hurt or where we hurt anyone perceived as coming too close to revealing sins committed. People are pros when this issue is brought to light.

We can say that we are not the same persons that we were years ago, and we would be right in saying so. We are new creatures created in Messiah (Christ) unto good works. We can approach this as not having any more to do with anyone who might disclose our sins. We cut ourselves out of the lives of others, or others cut us from their lives. We hide in shame, just like Adam and Eve did in the garden when they hid themselves.

But I am not advocating confiding our sins to everyone we meet. We must be sure the people we confide in can be trusted not to use the information we give them as weapons against us to get what they want at our expense. This does happen, and the information is used to blame, condemn, and accuse so that we are often left being hurt worse than before we confided in someone. This creates an unhealthy fear as well, because thereafter we will rarely reach out to get the help needed in order to get better.

How is this debilitating fear overcome? Paul is an expert in using the sins of his past to further the kingdom of Messiah (Christ). We're going to learn from his life and the lives of others and then apply those lessons to ourselves.

Let's begin with the scenario of a teenager who killed a person while driving home drunk. Not a day in the life of this young man goes by that he forgets what his experience cost the lives of people he did not know—and the cost to himself. He no longer drinks. While in jail, he was approached by the parents whose son he killed. They asked if he would be willing to speak in schools about the heartbreak of drinking and what it can cost. He has spoken in several schools about his whole experience and is now an advocate against getting drunk. During his talks, he strengthens young people in their resolve not to drink and suggests ways to deal with temptation. Using his past doesn't debilitate him. He has used it to protect others from the same mistakes. Paul did the same with his life.

Look at Acts 26:9–11. In these verses, Paul describes his life before Yeshua (Jesus). He doesn't stop there. He uses his past life to glorify Yeshua (Jesus) in bringing forth His forgiveness, compassion, and mercy. God used Paul despite his past to bring salvation to others. Yeshua (Jesus) doesn't stop using Paul in these two areas. He also uses Paul to dissuade others from committing sins. Paul had an epiphany that he was delivered from his past, that he was more than his past, that he could use his past to discourage sin, and that he could preach salvation to humankind—which is what he did for the rest of his life. We can do the same.

Look at Colossians 2:13. This is true of all of us. Prior to receiving Yeshua (Jesus), we are all dead in transgressions. After receiving Yeshua (Jesus) as our Lord and Savior, we are all made alive, having been forgiven. Do you know what this means for us? *That we don't have to live in fear of our past.* We can give God the glory for our deliverance—not only for us but for everyone. When people admit divorce, alcohol addiction, drug addiction, adultery, or any other past sins, they have the knowledge to discourage or prevent others from going down the same road. Read James 5:20. Those of us who admit to the sins in our past can be a source of encouragement to others in bringing the messages of deliverance and salvation.

I have had the privilege of speaking with people who have been delivered from a number of sins who now give messages of salvation and hope to vast numbers of people. I'm not referring to small sins here. I have spoken to people delivered from heroin addiction, people who have committed murder, and people with sexual addictions who know the value of getting and staying clean. There is a difference between someone who talks about smoking, its dangers, and how to get and stay delivered and someone else who had the same habit but who never says a word to anyone out of fear of being found out. One lives in fear. The other lives in freedom. With deliverance, Yeshua (Jesus) often positions us to attend to other people.

Receiving and giving forgiveness is one of many methods the Lord uses to help us and others discover His freedom. Then we can work to help others with the same or similar problems, thereby serving both the Lord and humankind. Whenever we pray, bless, encourage, call, text, give an unexpected gift, visit, or mail something such as a greeting card to enhance our journey and that of others in a relationship with the Lord, we become His servants.

Consider what a servant does. Not all servants serve in the same capacity, but all serve. Some servants are overseers to make sure everything is done in a correct order. Other servants are fathers, mothers, sons, daughters, students, employees, and employers. Servants do a variety of tasks, such as set tables, chauffeur cars, bring in wood to stoke a fire, make beds, do laundry, drive trucks, fly planes, perform surgery, perform dental work, herd cattle—the list goes on. This is good news, because each of us is designed by the Lord to serve Him and one another. To be in the Lord's service can consist of small gestures.

Have you ever witnessed someone receiving a hug while he or she was distraught? Have you ever said, "Smile, it can't be that bad!" Perhaps you have thanked someone for working on the Sabbath who was capable of handling an emergency. To be in the service of the Lord is to be available to Him on a moment's notice—and it doesn't have to be any more involved than saying, "Have a great day." When we are able and our hearts are prepared, He may call on us for bigger jobs.

During my stay in Spokane, Washington, I noticed that many people were homeless by choice. These same people would get out their signs, stating their need of help. I gathered a team to put together food bags to give out. The bags included bottled water, snacks, and gift cards to local eating establishments. Then, in a separate bag, we put winter wear for the colder weather, toothbrushes, toothpaste, small soaps, and so on. For me, handing out the bags came closer to being obedient to the Lord when He instructs us to give people food, clothing, and water. For the most part, people were very grateful. One man stood out more than all the others, and I had to know his story.

I had watched this homeless man for several weeks whenever I came to town. I learned that he was serving the Lord right where he was and performing his service well. Once a week, he stood on a corner, not asking for anything. He wasn't always on the same corner but always on a corner. That was the first thing I became aware of. While standing there, he faithfully held a piece of cardboard with a message on it—a new note written down every day. His delivery of communication was absolutely delightful. He would stand up, wave, and smile, as if you were his very best friend in the world, showing his sign every time people appeared on his corner. He was the happiest homeless man I had ever seen. That's when I made the decision to meet him.

First, I put a food bag together for him. Then I gathered up an eraser board with the pens and eraser he could use to write as many signs as he needed without having to always find new cardboard for his messages. With my vehicle parked, I walked up to him. As I approached, he smiled and waved with his communication for the day. I offered him the food bag and the eraser board. He turned down all that I had brought for him. He was very humble and polite as he declined. As my interest grew, I had to know why he was doing what he was doing.

The man explained that he was on a mission from the Lord. He was to do nothing during the weekly day he spent on a given corner except to brighten people's day as they drove or walked by. He was also not to accept anything from anyone, no matter what was offered, until his day on the corner was finished. I didn't know where to find him when he was finished, so he never accepted what I had for him. But there is more to his story.

A lot of homeless people stop holding out their help-needed signs when the police drive by. The first time a police officer pulled over to the happy homeless man, he couldn't get into trouble with his signs because he wasn't soliciting for anything. He even managed to brighten days for policemen. The happy homeless man was in service to the Lord, and he made a difference on a street corner. I hope he is doing well. Each of us is a miracle belonging to the Lord.

We're more than a miracle to Him. We are one of His crowns and a source of His joy. His joy is to be shared. The Lord gives us our span of life, skill, and aptitude. A question we can ask ourselves is, what are some ways we serve Him using the abilities He has bestowed on us concerning receiving and giving forgiveness? Everyone has at least one skill. Remember—we are part of the body of Yeshua (Jesus)—a foot, a hand, an eye, an ear, and so on.

Each one of us can recognize a person who sings beautifully and acknowledge someone who acts well and becomes a movie star. We take note of a great author. But here's a surprise to many: each of us has at least one outstanding efficiency given to us from Yeshua (Jesus) Himself! Everyone has been given a natural ability to do something well for Him from Him! Let's get a few ideas that pertain to us in our given personality. How do we know we are in line with qualities He has bestowed in us? Because it rings true with us, like a song we really enjoy.

What do we do if we find we want to have a talent belonging to someone else? Well, here's at least one idea: we can acquire the knowledge necessary to achieve a desired talent that we currently do not own. Think about trading money for lessons or otherwise becoming educated in the talents we desire. We may discover along the way, though, that we really didn't want that talent after all because it does not fit our personality. This is similar to wearing someone else's shoes that fit either too tight or too loose.

As we discover our fit, we will naturally adapt to our talent or talents and become satisfied in our roles. Each of us can become aware of our talents and succeed in putting them to use for the Lord while we continue to grow in our relationship with Him. Putting to use one outstanding talent—or many of them—will be an aid to our personal life and the lives of those we come into contact with. Try to come up with at least one talent that rightfully belongs to you from Yeshua (Jesus) concerning the topic of forgiveness.

Let's approach the topic of our rights. What happens when a country is at risk of losing freedom? The citizens of that country fight for their right to remain free. What happens when our right to become or stay free is threatened? We stand and fight for the rights given to us from Yeshua (Jesus). What would we say if Satan were standing in front of us, demanding that we not forgive someone who has hurt us? Our first response would be to remind him that Yeshua (Jesus) is our Lord. Secondly, we would announce to Satan that whomever he didn't want us to forgive is forgiven, if for no other reason than to fight to remain free from bitterness. We will then say something like, "Be gone!" We recognize first who is sitting on the throne and who isn't. We know who our Lord is and who He isn't. Putting Satan in his place is part of our glorious journey laid out for us by Yeshua (Jesus).

Now we are ready to move to the next department.

**\*For Small Groups**

Give everyone an opportunity to discuss rewards people enjoy receiving.

- When the temptation to pick up bitterness, wrath, and so on—either toward ourselves or others—occurs, what are some tools we can use to no longer embrace those unhealthy emotions?

- What are unique traits of tribulation, temptation, troubles, tests, and trials?

- How can we defeat unhealthy fear so that we are not crippled by it?

- Do you have an idea of what your talents are in serving the Lord?

- Where do you stand when your God-given kingdom rights are being threatened?

# Chapter 18

## Anger of Others Directed at Us and Themselves

In the previous department, the issue of our own anger against ourselves and against others was addressed. Here we will deal with the anger of others directed toward us and back at themselves.

When people do not confess sins against them, anger and bitterness take up residence within their minds toward us. We may sow good seed, good works, and good words into the life of another and yet reap their bitterness, wrath, and so on. Sometimes wrath really becomes apparent when we have sinned against someone.

The question is, why would people feel angry toward us when we are trying to express compassion toward the plight of others in acknowledgment of our sins against them? The answer is usually twofold. One is that people have not gotten to a good place concerning the sins we committed against them, which results in bitterness, wrath, and so on toward us. The second is that people haven't gotten over the sins they themselves committed against someone, which results in bitterness, wrath, and so on toward themselves.

Let's look at the first answer. When we sin against another, we need to place ourselves in front of the person we have hurt. We cannot allow ourselves to condone our conduct by saying, "I can't deal with seeing you in the pain that my sin against you caused. I have to get out of here." We must see this through to completion. There can be no vindications or exemptions on our part that allow us to ignore our responsibility to help those whom we have hurt.

Picture us standing in front of someone we have hurt. The person we have sinned against is going to confess our sin(s) without condemnation or judgment against us. He or she will say something like, "When the sin of ___ (sin identified) was committed, so much turmoil came into my life. My life was a mess spiritually, emotionally, mentally, and physically because of the sins you committed against me. There was a time when I felt bitter and angry toward you and the sins committed. I have asked (am asking) the Lord through His blood, compassion, mercy, forgiveness, and His agape love for you to come and cover the sin(s) involved that were committed against me at that time. I choose not feel bitter about those incidents any longer. I have also asked the Lord to live inside me with His heart. He answered my prayer, and I have Yeshua (Jesus) living within me. I have the heart of Yeshua (Jesus) toward you in place of the rage I held against you for so long. I have His character of forgiveness, compassion, and kindness toward you." Completing the above exercise will bring healing for the person or persons we have sinned against as they grow in the characteristics of Yeshua. Let's now consider sins people commit that result in anger toward themselves. This exercise is much like the earlier one dealing with anger toward ourselves. Like us, when others do not confess their sins, anger and bitterness take up residence within their minds toward themselves. People in this group are going to confess their sin(s) without condemnation or judgment against themselves. They will say something like, "When the sin of ____ (sin identified) was committed, a lot of pain was brought into my life. Because of my sins against you, a lot of pain was also brought into your life. The lives of both of us were deeply affected on several levels. I once felt bitterness and anger toward myself for the sins I committed. I have asked (am asking) the Lord through His blood, compassion, mercy, forgiveness, and His love for me to come and cover the sin(s) committed. I'll not feel bitter about those incidents any longer. I have also asked the Lord to live inside me with His heart. He answered my prayer, and I have Yeshua (Jesus) living within me. I have the heart of Yeshua (Jesus) toward myself instead of the hatred I held toward myself for so long. I have His character of forgiveness, compassion, and kindness toward myself. I'll do what I can to make a good difference in your life from now on. I am sorry."

Tears can often be anticipated. Reality does not magically disappear with forgiveness. Receiving forgiveness is wholesome for both parties, the one who needs forgiveness and the one who forgives. Giving forgiveness without denying the truth about pain being deposited into our lives and the lives of others is healing when bitterness gives way to compassion.

But what are we to do when someone insists on hanging on to bitterness? People sometimes continue to spew a sewage hose of anger all over us, even after we have done all we can do to confess (agree) that the sins were committed. We have taken the steps to hear them out. We have repented of the hurt brought into their lives through our sins by seeing that we never bring additional pain of a similar nature. We also see that we don't bring additional pain through accusations of any kind, including perceiving them to be unforgiving. When people persist on clinging to their unhealthy anger toward us, we may have to end the relationship. We can pray the blood of Yeshua (Jesus) over the persons in this situation.

We can pray the blood over our perceptions as well and receive forgiveness; however, if we stay in a relationship under someone's perpetual anger, we become like a healthy plant placed into a pot of poison. Here's why. People filled with bitterness, wrath, unhealthy anger, clamor, slander, and malice do not recognize these characteristics as sins. There is no acknowledgment of unhealthy emotions as sins that need to be owned, confessed, repented of, and forgiveness received for. We are not to continue to allow others to deposit those sins into our lives.

When excessive destructive anger is directed at us, we may have to step away or out of a relationship for a time. We can still pray for healing of the damaged emotions and pray the blood of Yeshua (Jesus) to cover those sins. Read Galatians 5:20. Pay attention to outbursts of anger. This is one of the deadly sins.

People are sometimes blind to sins like bitterness and unhealthy anger because they get too caught up in shifting responsibility to someone else when dealing with these negative emotions. They are too bound up blaming, accusing, condemning, and justifying their own behavior. These people are not responsible for the pain brought to their lives through the sins we committed against them, but they are responsible for their own healing of that pain.
Yeshua (Jesus) has also forgiven all bitterness, wrath, unhealthy anger, clamor, slander, and malice of others toward us. In Ephesians 4:31, we are instructed to let that *entire* list be put away.

"Entire" includes each of the four categories—anger against ourselves, anger toward others, anger of others toward us, and anger toward themselves.

What do we do when we feel anger against God?


**\*For Small Groups**

Give everyone an opportunity to discuss the four categories of anger thus far: anger against self, anger against others, anger of others directed at us, and anger of others directed at themselves.

o   What do you perceive as putting away unhealthy emotions?

o   Does facing potential loss of relationships sometimes prevent us from disallowing people to continue to spew hurtful comments to us?

# Chapter 19

## Anger against God

Because of God's attributes of being all-seeing, all-knowing, all-powerful, and all God all the time, many people are moved to anger against Him. Let's consider some possible reasons why.

People contend with God when He does not stop, intervene, interrupt, or prevent something evil from happening. After all, He is God and is all-powerful. Now, on top of this fact, add the times He *did* prevent evil in the life of someone else but not in our own. We read about the flood in Genesis. We read about the destruction of Sodom and Gomorrah. We even read about individuals like Abimelech in Genesis. Because of the integrity in the heart of Abimelech, God kept him from sinning against Abraham, Sarah, and Himself. God did not let Abimelech touch Sarah. What gives? Why did God prevent evil in this situation and at other times allow evil to take place? Read Genesis 20:1–11.

In Genesis 1:11, Abraham made an assumption that no connection existed between God and Abimelech, which clearly was not the case. Evil did not take place because of the relationship that did exist. Abimelech did listen to the voice of God, and He was obedient to the instructions given to him. The prevention of evil in our lives and the lives of others takes place when there is an interdependent relationship between the Holy Spirit and people.

Let's take a closer look at Yeshua (Jesus). Pick up the KoS bag and write on labels "His attributes" and "His description." Stick them on the bag. Put enough white cotton balls on the inside of

the bag to represent each of His qualities. I'll begin
a list.

- God
- Compassionate
- Creator
- Kindhearted
- Lord
- Humble
- All-Seeing
- All-Knowing
- All-Powerful
- Gentle
- Patient
- Beloved
- Agape Love
- Teacher
- Redeemer
- Forgiver
- Holy
- Blameless
- Beyond Reproach
- Light
- True (speaks truth)
- Faithful
- Full of Grace
- Merciful

Look closely at the bag with all of the white cotton balls inside and His character.

Next, pick up the DoD bag. On labels, write the following list, and then stick the labels on the DoD bag. Put enough black cotton balls on the inside of the DoD bag to represent each item listed.

- Evil Deeds
- Unhealthy Anger
- Hostile
- Wrath
- Dead in Transgressions
- Immoral
- Malice
- Impurity
- Slander
- Passion
- Clamor
- Abusive Speech
- Evil Desire
- Bitterness
- Greed
- Idolatry

Look closely at both bags. Remember, we reside in the KoS bag. As we look at the bag, take note that no darkness exists in the bag with the white cotton balls. Read 1 John 1:5. There are no black cotton balls in the baggie with the white cotton balls.

There are a lot of lessons here. One lesson we are going to see is a clear picture of us in Yeshua (Jesus).

The statement is made that there is therefore now no condemnation for those who are *in* Messiah (Christ) Yeshua (Jesus). As we look at the KoS baggie, the truth that we are forgiven is easy to see. Yeshua (Jesus) has no unhealthy anger or wrath toward us. When in doubt, we can check it out. Study the KoS baggie, and discover His attributes concerning us. We have a picture of who we are in Yeshua (Jesus).

Let's look at an additional picture of what Yeshua (Jesus) in us looks like. In Colossians 1:20, a mystery is revealed that Yeshua (Jesus) in us is the hope of glory. We will never be God or Yeshua (Jesus), but we can become like Yeshua (Jesus) in His attributes. When we are compassionate, kindhearted, gentle, patient, and forgiving of one another, Yeshua (Jesus) is living in us through His Holy Spirit. As we meditate on the KoS bag, we have more of a complete picture of us in Yeshua (Jesus) and Him in us.

Another lesson we are going to look at is that God is not - nor will ever be - the creator of evil. From Genesis to Revelation, we will never find any instructions to us from God to ignore the Sabbath, dishonor our parents, steal, commit adultery, be a false witness, covet what belongs to our neighbor, and so on.

We do find in His Word, though, directives to honor the Sabbath, honor our parents, labor with hands in order to give, remain faithful in marriage, be a true witness, keep our hands off of what belongs to another, and so on. Evil often takes place when we or others do not obey His instructions and commandments.

During times of disobedience, Yeshua (Jesus) is not in the proper place as our Lord.

When He is our Lord, we are obedient to Him and His instructions. Disobedience to God is first seen in Genesis in the garden. God instructed the man (Adam) not to eat from the tree of the knowledge of good and evil. He told the man (Adam) what would happen if he did. Here we have the fall of man.

This illustration explains why evil happens, but why does God allow it to take place? We may never know all His reasons in this life, but we can know some of them. Our disobedience often leads us to welcoming Yeshua (Jesus) as our Lord (we are ready to become obedient to His instructions) and our Savior. This is a piece of information we can know. Read Galatians 2:16. Not one of us is saved by obedience to all the laws of God, because not one person - except for Yeshua (Jesus) - was faithful in pleasing God in everything. Another piece of information we can learn as to why God allows evil to take place is that He wants no one to perish. Read 2 Peter 3:9.

Let's see the patience of Yeshua (Jesus) in action. This story begins with God creating someone He sends here to earth. The person sent has been instructed not to steal from another person - but he does steal. From here, we'll see why His patience is so important. Yeshua (Jesus) begins pleading with the thief to come to Him.
Remember, He left the ninety-nine who didn't do wrong to seek out the one who did. We can see Him talking with the thief, saying something like, "I plead with you to come to Me. I'll not turn you away. Please acknowledge your sin before Me. I'll forgive you. Ask Me to be your

Lord. I'll teach you and provide a job for you. In earnest ask Me to be your Savior. I'll save you. Come to Me. I still love you. Before your enemies I'll be your advocate. Above all else, please come to Me before you die. I want to have you with Me for eternity. I don't want to lose you forever." God is patient because He is aware of eternal consequences.

God promises to dry all our tears so that our sorrow lasts but a short time in view of eternity. He sees eternal losses and wants no one to perish where suffering does not come to an end. The patience and forgiveness of Yeshua (Jesus) is seen clearly in Luke 23:39-43 between Himself and one of the criminals. In the book of Luke, Satan uses the crucifixion of one criminal as a source to have abuse hurled at Yeshua (Jesus) bound in bitterness, wrath, and malice. Using the same verses, Yeshua (Jesus) uses the crucifixion to teach us about Himself, His qualities, and His character. His nature was and is forgiving, tenderhearted, and compassionate for us.

As we learn more about Yeshua (Jesus), anger against God dissipates. Love and adoration for God enters our hearts, minds, and spirits.

We are now departing from the Town of Igloos. By this time in our journey, not only are we equipped to receive and grant forgiveness - we are ready to go beyond forgiveness.

**\*For Small Groups**

Give everyone an opportunity to discuss the story of Abimelech and the lessons learned.

o  What are your thoughts concerning living the attributes of Yeshua (Jesus) through us?

o  Why is the patience of God so important? Why does is last so long?

o  What are some methods of making transitions from negative to positive emotions toward God?

# Chapter 20

# This Thing Called Love

As we leave the Town of Igloos, look up and take notice. We have broken through the avalanche. Some melting is taking place. Some sunshine is peeking through. Temperatures are somewhere around fifty or sixty degrees Fahrenheit. We are ready to continue on our journey. One stop we will make is at the Agape Love Inn, where we will learn how to love.

Read Luke 6:27(a). Here we are instructed to love our enemies. An enemy is someone who has sinned against us. Prior to the sin that took place, there was no enemy. You could have been the best of friends with this person; he or she could have been a relative or someone you did not even know. No sin equals no enemy. There is nothing to forgive, because sin had not taken place. But both before *and after* sin takes place, we are instructed to agape love.

There are three types of love. One representation of love is phileo. Everybody needs a friend, and this is phileo love. Another variety of love is eros. This is sexual love. Eros is blessed by God within the confines of marriage. Eros is mutual sexual love between man and woman. Eros is often blessed by having children. In Genesis, God blessed Adam and Eve and told them to go forth and multiply.

Then there is agape love. This is the kind of love with which we are instructed to love one another.

Read John 13:34–35. When Yeshua (Jesus) told us to love one another as He has loved us (without sin), He was referring to agape love. He Himself never sinned against us or anyone else. Agape love is how we are instructed to love one another first. In other words, we love one another by not sinning against one another.

When we do not sin against one another, we are not enticing anyone else to sin. Plus, we do not allow others to attract us to sin, thereby not sinning against ourselves. We do not invite sin into our lives through ourselves or others.

Read 1 Timothy 6:11 and 2 Timothy 2:22. There are times when it's okay to run. We are to run from sin. Don't dillydally with it. Don't shilly-shally with sin—just run. Remember, when the Lord instructs us in His Word to run from something, He also tells us what to run toward and embrace. His Word instructs us to chase after righteousness, faith, (agape) love, peace, godliness, and so on. When we follow His teachings, we are not running toward a problem—we are running from a problem toward a solution. We know what pursuing agape love is. We know what a peaceful atmosphere is. We know how to emulate a godly lifestyle.

What does chasing after righteousness resemble? After all, we're not likely to pursue something if we're not sure what it is or how it benefits us.

Righteousness is doing that which is right as defined by God. To agape love our enemies is to do what Yeshua (Jesus) says to do and considers a righteous act. Righteousness can also be determined by obedience. However, compliance to God is not obedience alone; it must be accompanied by the heart of God. Another way to express righteousness or agape love is trying to stop or protect others from sinning. Read James 5:19–20.

When we have sinned against someone and see someone else considering taking the same route, we jump in and say, "Please don't do that. Painful consequences are involved that you know nothing about, and we don't want that experience for you or your family. Some of those consequences will be with you for the rest of your life. Those choices are not the way to handle the issues you are facing. We'll figure out solutions that work, just in a different way."

What are we to do once sin has taken place? We are still to agape love those who have sinned against us. We are to bring the compassion, forgiveness, mercy, and kindness of the Lord to the person or persons who wronged us. If you have love (agape love of God) for one another, then you are truly His disciples. If you have seen a picture of Yeshua (Jesus) holding up the man who drove the nails into His feet and hands, you understand agape love and righteousness.

Read Colossians 1:19–23. We are going to look at what the verses are referring to when they say "through the blood" and what "the faith" means shortly. Pay attention to Colossians 1:21 that you (all of us) "were formerly"—*were* and *formerly* are past-tense words.

Write out Colossians 1:21. "And although you were formerly alienated and hostile in mind, engaged in evil deeds," and stick it on the outside of the DoD bag. Take three black cotton balls and place them into the DoD bag. One of these represents "formerly alienated," another represents "hostile in mind,' and the third represents "engaged in evil deeds."

Write out verse 1:22, and stick this verse on the outside of the KoS bag. Take three white cotton balls and place them into the KoS bag. One of these represents "you presented before Him holy." Another represents "you are blameless." The third represents "you are beyond reproach."

Let's address what "through the blood" is. Have you ever gone through a tunnel? You start out on one side of the tunnel, go through it, and come out the other side. With regard to the cross, we begin on this side of the cross as Yeshua (Jesus) deals with our sins.

In essence, here's what would have happened if Yeshua (Jesus) hadn't risen from the dead: preaching would be in vain, our faith would be in vain, we would be false witnesses of God, our faith would be worthless, we would still be in our sins, and our loved ones that have passed away would have perished. The writer goes on in verse 20 to let us know that Messiah (Christ) has risen from the dead and that He is the first fruits of those who are asleep. We will see why His resurrection is so important to us.

His death deals with our eternal state and enables us to reside with Him eternally. His resurrection deals with His authority about who He is and who we are from His perspective. Read 1 Corinthians 15:12–20. These verses relate just how important the resurrection of Yeshua (Jesus) is. We go through the blood of Yeshua (Jesus) and come out on the other side of the cross to His resurrected state of being, where we are announced holy, blameless, forgiven, and so on.

Besides the list given above, going back to Colossians, we all need the living Lord Messiah (Christ) in order for Him to do the "now" in

Colossians 1:22. "Yet He has *now* reconciled you in His fleshly body through death in order to present you before Him holy, blameless, and beyond reproach." Messiah (Christ) in His resurrected state now has the authority to announce to you and me that we are holy before Him. An unrisen person cannot give new life or do the "now."

Next, let's understand what "the faith" is pointing to; otherwise, how will we know we are continuing in the faith?

To continue in the faith is to proclaim His death and His resurrection and to agree with what He says about us in Colossians 1:22. Another aspect of righteousness is believing what the Word of God says. Read verse 1:23, as there is a contingency to verse 1:22. The stipulation is *if you (we) continue in the faith*.

To continue in the faith is twofold. The faith includes the death and resurrection of Yeshua (Jesus). Colossians 1:14 states that we have been granted redemption and forgiveness of our sins. Take another label, write out Colossians 1:14. "in whom we have redemptions, the forgiveness of sins." and stick this verse on the outside of the KoS bag. Next, take two white cotton balls, and put them inside the KoS bag, which represents where you reside.

When God redeemed us, He reclaimed ownership by delivering us from the kingdom of darkness to the kingdom of His Son. In the garden before the fall of man, God had full ownership of man. After the fall of man, sin took place, and God no longer had complete possession because sin separated God and His authority over man. In the Old Testament, provision was made through the sacrificial systems for man to be forgiven of sins. In the New Testament, through Yeshua (Jesus), provision is made for our sins to be forgiven. He didn't redeem us for our benefit alone. He redeemed us for His purposes. Read 2 Corinthians 5:18–20.

One of the objectives God had in giving us a ministry of reconciliation is for the heart of God to be understood—that He wants redemption for everyone who comes to Him—and to reestablish friendship between Himself and humans, including those who have sinned against us. The agape love of Yeshua (Jesus) contains within it several components. Yeshua (Jesus) doesn't stop with agape love. He continues to instruct us to do good.

It is time to continue on our trip until we arrive at our new destination.

### *For Small Groups

Give everyone an opportunity to discuss the agape love of God.

o  What are some ways righteousness can be presented so that the concept is not so vague?

o  Discuss what "through the blood" means.

o  Discuss continuing in "the faith."

o  What are some thoughts concerning reconciliation and redemption?

# Chapter 21

## This Thing Called Good

Let's stop for some refreshment at the Good Doers Restaurant. Ephesians 2:10 offers some key things to understand about us. This single verse is packed with knowledge. One insight we derive is that we are the workmanship of God. All of us have seen good-quality workmanship and poor-quality workmanship. Since God has made us His workmanship, we are of excellent quality to carry out the good works He has laid out for us.

Another insight we can glean from Ephesians 2:10 is that we are created in Yeshua (Jesus). Look again at the KoS bag. It gives us a clear picture of who we are *in* Yeshua (Jesus). Colossians 1:28 and 2:10 both state that we are complete *in* Yeshua (Jesus).

The fact that we are made complete in Yeshua (Jesus) means we are well on our way toward acquiring the abilities and everything necessary to carry out His Word.

During springtime, many people are busy planting gardens. What makes for a successful garden? First, the weeds need to be taken out of the garden area. Then the soil needs to be turned over. People often use rotary plows or at least garden hoes. We give the soil added nutrition, and then seeds are bought and planted. The soil and seeds get watered. Weeds are pulled throughout the growing season. Finally, enjoyment of the food takes place. By this time in our journey, we are beings of beneficial workmanship of God made in Yeshua (Jesus) to do good works.

But just doing good works does not save us. Only Yeshua (Jesus) is our Savior. Good works are an outward expression of His living inside us and through us. We *in* Yeshua (Jesus) and Yeshua (Jesus) *in* us is what equips us to carry out His good works. What are good works defined by Yeshua (Jesus)? You will discover the answer coming up shortly. Let's define His meaning of good.

The meaning of good in the heart of God is for us to be a benefit to others. When we express kindness to others, we look for ways through the leading of the Holy Spirit to do good and enhance lives of others. Another discernment we gather from Ephesians 2:10 is that God created certain good works for us to walk in and carry out. Have you ever asked the question, "Why me?"

Why would any of us do good to someone else, especially when that someone has hurt us deeply? God placed each of us to reach out and express His heart and nature in the lives of others. People who have hurt us deeply need His forgiveness and compassion and to have works of goodness extended to them. We are His chosen vessels to bring Him into the lives of others. We are instructed to take every opportunity to do good to all humans (humankind) (Galatians 6:10).

We are also instructed to do good in Luke 6:27(b). "Do good to those who hate you." Doing good requires an action, like cooking a meal, washing the dishes, or doing the laundry. Doing something is not inactive or stagnant; it is active.

Not doing something may look like inaction, but it may in fact not be passive. Sometimes when we have sinned against someone, the person we sinned against might ask us to back off and leave them alone because they need time to heal. We respect the request, and our inaction is the action in place. The fact is, backing off and giving the person the time needed to heal is an action, even though it looks as if we are not doing anything. Our inaction is the good we are doing by respecting a person's need for time. We can pray for his or her continual healing while we are not in touch.

Before we continue to do good to someone who hates us, some guidelines must be put into place. First, we have to know the reasons and motives in our hearts as to why we are going to do good to our enemies. The reason is that we are instructed to do good by Yeshua (Jesus), as stated right in His Word. Secondly, we have to know the motive in our hearts as to why we are going to do good to our enemies.

Our motive is our heart check. Some instructors say, "Just do what He says. Just be obedient to His Word, and everything will work out." This teaching is not good instruction when our hearts are not in line with the heart of God and when we are obeying merely for the sake of obedience.

Prior to doing good to our enemies, what is our inner witness saying to us? "I'll do good to my enemy, but this doesn't feel right. I'll do this, but I don't really want to. I'll do this because I have to. I'm doing this to look good to other people, but if they only knew…I'll do this just to be obedient, but I'm feeling angry on the inside. I'll do this, but I'm going to let him or her have it when we're through! I'm doing this because I'm feeling guilty. I'm doing this, but I feel taken advantage of."

If our inner witness says anything that resembles or even comes close to any of the statements or feelings above, the time has not arrived to do good to our enemies. We are to be obedient and do good to our enemies *with the heart of God involved.*

Consider the motives of our heart. The time to do good to our enemy has come when our inner witness says, "I am doing this as an expression of the kindness, tender heart, and character of God, and I want to bless the life of my enemy." This is the time to do good to our enemy—not before. Here is a short story to illustrate.

Two friends, Shawna and Becky, each have some things that belong to them. Shawna wants her own things, but she also wants what belongs to Becky. So Shawna takes what belongs to Becky. After a time, the Lord speaks to Shawna, wanting her to give something back to Becky and add a little more, too. The gesture from the perspective of the Lord is to let Becky know that the injury caused by Shawna hasn't gone unnoticed and that He wants some healing to take place in her life. In obedience, Shawna brings forth a series of gifts for Becky. Becky decides it's okay for her to receive the gifts from Shawna, because she considered this to be Shawna's way of apologizing to Becky for what she had done.

All is well until Shawna comes back and accuses Becky, saying, "How dare you take advantage of me. How dare you look out for your own interests and not look out for *my* best interests. Yes, I offered those things, but you didn't have to take them. You're an awful person, Becky!"

Again, Becky is devastated. Dealing with issues that caused the first hurt was bad enough. Now, accusations have been added. Becky didn't realize that Shawna wasn't okay with her gesture toward her, or she wouldn't have accepted what

Shawna offered. Becky gave Shawna back her things.

Becky felt heartbroken. She realized that no agape love of God had been involved in Shawna's gesture. She had been driven by something, but it was not agape love. The driving force could have been guilt, anger, or obligation. Perhaps the driving force was one of compulsion or necessity, believing that she had to do *something*.

As it turns out, things are not any better with Shawna. Even though her things were returned, she realized she'd gone to Becky with the motive of saying hurtful things and causing her additional grief.

What happened? What went wrong? The answer is that the heart of God was not involved in Shawna's heart to begin with. This is what happened with Ananias and Sapphira.

Read Acts 5:1–10. Peter asks five questions: "Ananias, why has Satan filled your heart to lie to the Holy Spirit and keep back some of the price of the land? While it remained unsold, did it not *remain your own*? And after it was sold, was it not *under your control*? Why is it that you conceived this deed in your heart? You have not lied to men, but to God."

All Ananias and Sapphira had to do was to come clean and confess that they had changed their mind about how much they wanted to give after they sold the land. God and Peter would have been satisfied with their honest answer. This is why Peter asked, "While unsold, wasn't it *yours*? And after it was sold, wasn't it under *your* control?" Obedience without the heart of God invested leads to people getting hurt.

Draw another thermometer, and mark where you are at in the desire to show agape love of God to an enemy. If the mark is low, then wait until your heart is infused with His. If it is high and His heart is invested with yours, wait until He leads you in what to do. If you have an enemy who wants to show you a gesture of kindness because he or she has sinned against you, try to learn why the person wants to do something for you.

If someone cannot give you the reason for an act of kindness following the instructions of Yeshua (Jesus) with His heart invested, gently decline the gift being presented. In the above story about Shawna and Becky, had Becky known the feelings of her friend Shawna, she would not have accepted anything that was offered and avoided further pain.

Another heart check must be considered before we do good to our enemies. We must realize what we can do to keep ourselves a cheerful giver. We are to look out for our interests and the interests of others. Since God loves a cheerful giver, we need to make sure that we do not give to the point of overextension, which leads to anger and bitterness over feeling taken advantage of. God is content with what we give, even when we start out with nothing more than a greeting card.

Now, draw another thermometer, and mark the place indicating where you are ready to do good to your enemy. Mark another place that represents your motives. Mark a third place that represents what you can cheerfully give. The marks you place on the thermometer are to be used as a guide.

The next stop on our journey will be at the bountiful blessings of words. The next instruction we receive from the Lord is to bless those who curse you.

**\*For Small Groups**

Give everyone an opportunity to discuss doing good.

o   What are some weeds that may need to be pulled out of our garden before we do good to someone?

o   Can you understand that inaction can be an action?

o   What are some thoughts on motives?

o   What are some thoughts on heart checks?

# Chapter 22

## This Thing Called Blessing

There are two key words in Luke 6:28: "bless" and "curse." The word "bless" in this context means to speak well of someone. When we bless someone, we are saying healing words that build character. To curse someone, on the other hand, is to say hurtful words that defile character. In other words, blessing is saying good things about or to someone while cursing is speaking ill to or about someone.

James 3:8 gives us a warning straightaway that our tongues are full of deadly poison. With the words of our mouth outside of Yeshua (Jesus), we cannot tame our tongues. With our speech, we can noxiously injure others, and in turn, we can be profoundly damaged by others.

Yeshua (Jesus) tells us in His Word that as the world hated Him, so there are times when the world will hate us, because we are *in* the world but not *of* the world. His Word also tells us that when men revile us falsely on account of Yeshua (Jesus), we are to rejoice because we have a great reward waiting for us in heaven. He will see to it that our recompense will have equality based on our words and deeds to Him and His kingdom.

Our rewards will not always be the same as what we receive in this life. We see this principle in the life of Paul in 1 Corinthians 4:12, where he says when they are reviled, they bless; when persecuted, they endure; and when slandered, they overcome the animosity of others shown to them.

By this, we learn what Paul and his companions did when faced with the attitudes of others. We are also going to learn some methods of managing our responses, because we can learn to do the same as Paul and the people he traveled with.

Each of us can speak well of others when we have been treated well. We can also speak well of others who are no longer in our lives but who were a blessing to us while they were. Anyone special to us who has died is often remembered with fond memories and is spoken well of. But we are also called to bless (say something good) to or about someone who speaks ill of us (when reviled, we bless). Words spoken that create hurt in our hearts, minds, and spirits is being cursed by words. This is a tough challenge, because many people get caught up in being reviled and simply revile back.

Read 1 Corinthians 3:3 and Galatians 5:20. We can bite, devour, and consume one another, speaking poison for poison, like returning insult for insult. The point is not whether or not we are to bless when reviled. The question is what to say to someone who is saying or has said mean, spiteful, hurtful words and from whom venom directed at us pours. We are still called to bless without lying against the truth. The task at hand is even more complicated when someone says all kinds of hurtful words yet claims Yeshua (Jesus) as the Lord and Savior. We need a little extra help here.

We can thank Yeshua (Jesus) in His provision of how to bless when reviled. I was asked about this very dilemma by someone very close to me. She called me and said, "I invested my heart and the heart of the Lord to be kindhearted to a woman who had hurt me. I wanted to bless her life. I know that was my motive. An act of kindness was intended. When I returned home a few days later, that same woman wrote me a letter with all kinds of hurtful statements and accusations against me. I was in tears over that letter. I still am, and that was over two years ago. I just don't know how to shake this. I know I'm supposed to bless and not curse. I just don't know how or what to do." The enemy was trying to pound this woman into the ground—and almost succeeded. I said almost. Yeshua (Jesus) won the victory.

The first step we took was to guide my friend to study both the DoD and the KoS bags. Her initial triumph came when she realized the words written to her containing bitterness, wrath, anger, malice, abusive speech, and accusations against her did not come from Yeshua (Jesus). The next action we took was to pray for the blood protection of Yeshua (Jesus) to cover the hurtful situation and those pain-filled words. We also prayed for healing of the damaged emotions for both parties involved. The next engagement we did was to receive healing words from the Lord.

Words of healing from scripture in opposition to the words of the enemy are what we searched out and chose to believe over and above the lies of the enemy. Some of the statements were from Romans 15:14, through which she was reminded that she is full of goodness and filled with information, able to advise that she would no longer accept such communication in the future. In Ephesians 2:10, my friend recalled that she is a new creature created in Yeshua (Jesus) for good works. She recollected that her offering was intended to be a blessing. Then an additional step was considered. This step involved saying something kind about the woman who inflicted the damaging words rather than cursing in return. This is a step in blessing—and where the rubber meets the road.

I took my friend shopping because she needed to find a place to start. I had her pick out two cards. One was a thank-you card. She was to discover the best one she could find, one that she would want to receive for herself. The second card she was to choose was a thinking-of-you card. After we arrived home, my friend retrieved the second card and wrote on it, "Those were hurtful words you wrote to me (speaking the truth in love), but you are still a nice person when you want to be." She wrote at least one nice thing to say about the woman who had hurt her instead of returning a curse. She is waiting to speak with her friend in person about how to communicate with her in the future.

I obtained the thank-you card and wrote in it. At the top of the card, I wrote the name of my friend. At the bottom I wrote words similar to Matthew 5:45, saying, "Thank you for being kind to the righteous and the unrighteous. Your Lord and Savior, Yeshua (Jesus)."

My friend has both cards tucked away. One reminds her of the time she broke the curse of hurtful words by not retaliating so much as it depended on her. The second card reminds her of the thankfulness of the Lord concerning her reaction.

Here is another story of how a different woman handled her situation. This woman received not one but two back-to-back hateful letters. As soon as the woman recognized the venom coming from the letters, she tore them up. Next, she was on the phone with a florist and had flowers with a card, balloon, and candy bar delivered to the woman who had written such ugly words to her. On the card, she wrote, "I'm sorry you were having a bad day. I hope these lift your spirits."

Actions like the illustrations above confound the enemy. The woman who wrote the letters knew the words she was writing were going to cause emotional pain. She wrote them intentionally to upset the woman she wrote to. This woman may not understand why she received flowers from her; however, she does understand that she did not receive injury for injury. She didn't receive insult for insult. The kindness of Yeshua (Jesus) came through.

Take a look at how we might deal with someone immediately in our proximity who spouts off angry, belittling words. Consider carrying two identical small cards. On one side of the cards, write at least one verse such as Colossians 3:12(b), where we are instructed to put on a heart of compassion, kindness, humility, gentleness, and patience. On the other side of the cards, write at least one verse such as Colossians 3:8, where we are instructed to put away unhealthy anger, wrath, malice, slander, and abusive speech from our mouths. When we are confronted with an angry person, pull out the cards, and give one of them to the person who is displaying a temper. Make sure both parties read both sides. This action often interrupts the attack. If the angry person persists in treating us badly, we are free to dismiss ourselves until a later time.

Draw a thermometer, and mark how well equipped you feel you are in speaking well of others when you are reviled. Mark another place on the thermometer indicating your ability to talk with an angry person.

In 1 Corinthians 4:12, Paul also speaks of enduring when persecuted. When Paul and his companions were harassed with ill treatment, they continued to carry on. In Acts 14:19–20, we learn that Paul was stoned to the point of death. That is some harsh treatment! But Paul got up and headed off to another place. What kept him going? He was determined to bring the message of salvation through Yeshua (Jesus). In his heart, Paul was acutely aware of the value of man. Yeshua (Jesus) considers all of humankind to be of such value. He died for our sins so that we would be with Him eternally. He rose for our justification.

There are times when Paul's rewards equaled what he gave out. During these times, Paul and others related the message of the gospel, and people came to Yeshua (Jesus) as their Lord and Savior. Yeshua (Jesus) forgave us completely through His death and life. We are to trade away our feelings of bitterness toward ourselves and others and embrace feelings of forgiveness and kindness of Yeshua (Jesus) toward ourselves and others. The more we embrace His characteristics, the sooner we will eventually abandon ill feelings altogether. This is why we are instructed in His Word that as we were freely given to, we are to freely give.

We can freely give kindness without a string of bitterness, envy, or the sense of someone owing us attached. Freely giving to someone comes through the acknowledgment of who [God and Yeshua (Jesus)] gave to us first and what They gave to us. We in turn give to another. We have the ability and knowledge to put away bitterness. But how do we deal with the issue of envy?

Envy occurs when someone wants what another person has. Envy outside the control of the Holy Spirit causes people to sometimes take what belongs to another without regard to the consequences for the person they are taking from.

There are two types of envy. One consists of wanting the talents and abilities that someone else has. Statements such as, "I wish I could sing like she does" may be heard when envy is present. This kind of envy can be dealt with in a way that does not bring hurt into the life of another.

Envy comes from a perceived lack of not having what another person has. People who want to sing as well as someone they admire can go out and trade money for voice lessons. Envy disappears when we can acquire our own abilities not at the expense of another person. When this is achieved, we can applaud the accomplishments of others and include our own achievements as well.

I have a condition known as shaking palsy, and my nervous system is damaged. I have had to deal with envy a lot over the years. For the most part, Yeshua (Jesus) is in control; however, there have been days when I have felt envious.

I feel envious at times when someone can lift a cup of coffee or glass of water and not worry about spilling it. People who do not have hands that shake take it for granted and have no idea of the struggle involved. They are so blessed. I was feeling particularly envious of photographers who could hold a camera steady and just snap a clear picture. This area of my life changed forever with one bit of information, and envy was laid to rest.

I was attending a family reunion. Pictures were being taken, and at that time, I truly thought I would never be involved with photography—until I took notice of something. A brother-in-law of mine was also at the reunion, and he mounted a camera on a tripod. With a remote, he snapped off a number of pictures, and I realized I could do that. I've been involved with photography ever since. My abilities have vastly improved. I communicate with one sister of mine on a consistent basis to discuss techniques. What I once envied, I now celebrate with others. We can trade our money for abilities. So, go for it.

There is another side of envy that needs to be put to rest. Sometimes we can sense that a person is envious of our skills. When this happens, the time has come to stand up and assist in discovering at least one ability belonging to the envious person. The truth is that Yeshua (Jesus) endows everyone with at least one talent for His glory. Once that talent is discovered and a person begins to walk in it, envy gives way to a healthy disposition. We can assist in aiding people to walk in their own light provided by Yeshua (Jesus). We cannot change the feeling of a specific feeling; however, we can change the feeling we are feeling. Does this concept sound confusing? It isn't.

The feeling of sadness will always yield sadness. The feeling of joy will always constitute joy. While we cannot change the feeling of sadness in what it produces, we can change the feeling of sadness to a different feeling. Paul also alludes to this when he tells us that people said things about him and his companions that hurt their characters but that they overcame the animosity shown to them. Paul and his friends did not get tangled up in the feelings of enmity shown to them by the crowd. They maintained healthy feelings toward the people who were abusive toward them. The question is, how did Paul accomplish this? The answer is that Paul and his friends knew the entire truth, and they allowed themselves grow with it.

Paul gives a discourse to King Agrippa in Acts 26:9–11 wherein he describes his life prior to

Yeshua (Jesus) as his Lord and Savior. Guess what, people? We are all in the same boat! All of us were dead in transgressions and sin prior to accepting Yeshua (Jesus) as our Lord and Savior (Ephesians 2:1–3). All of us have past lives where Yeshua (Jesus) was not in authority. Instead of allowing our past lives to debilitate us, just agree that the life we had before Yeshua (Jesus) existed and involved sin.

Paul didn't stop with just his past life; he continued to what his life became during and after his encounter with Yeshua (Jesus). He described to Agrippa how his life was different. Read Acts 26:12–25. Paul spoke words of truth about the death and resurrection of Yeshua (Jesus) so that humankind could be saved. This was his present life.

Paul also has a future life, stated in 2 Timothy 4:8. People who knew me a long time ago would not know me today. Have you heard a person say, "I've got some exciting news! I received the Lord as my Savior!" Such announcements are times to rejoice; however, making such statements does not mean the Lord becomes Lord of our whole life overnight. A relationship takes times to build. A person can be a believing Christian for a number of years and still be an infant in his or her relationship with the Lord if continual development does not take place.

For the Lord to become Lord over our behavior, our thought life, our speech, our emotional life, our treatment of one another, and so on, time is needed. As we give more of ourselves over to the Lord, we do not need to become defensive. When our past is brought up, we can just agree and say, "What you said is true, but that was before Yeshua (Jesus) was Lord in that area of my life."

Just like Paul, we have a past life that is different from our present life, and all of us have a future life. Draw a thermometer, and place a mark on it that represents how equipped you are when people bring up your past.

Now, let's talk about overcoming slander when people talk about us and our sins of the past. We might as well take the Word of God seriously. His Word states in Exodus 34:6–7 that when we sin or others sin against us, God does forgive iniquity, transgression, and sin; however, the iniquity of fathers is brought into the lives of their children and grandchildren. In other words, when sin is involved, people are going to talk about it up to three and four generations after the sins have been committed. We need to know how to deal with these situations so that they do not weaken us as believers when people talk about us or when we talk about others.

Slander occurs when we belittle the character of another person or when other people downgrade our character. We will follow the same model outlined in scripture to address the issue of slander. The pattern in scripture is to speak the whole truth. We were dead in transgressions and sin in our past before Yeshua (Jesus) became our Lord and Savior. We are different people today with Yeshua (Jesus) as Lord of our lives. Who we are in the present is not like who we will be in the future in Yeshua (Jesus). Slander is disarmed when we speak the whole truth.

In Romans 11:32, God Himself shuts up all in disobedience so that He can show mercy to all. One way God shows mercy is by using us to defend our faith, testimony, and belief in Him. Our faith is not for our benefit alone but also for the welfare of others. When a person we know is being slandered, we are to use that opportunity to defend the position of Yeshua (Jesus) from His perspective concerning another person. Remember the two quarters earlier in the book?

We are all blood bought and paid for, not bought with perishable silver or gold; however, the words of the Lord are more valuable than the purest silver or brightest gold. When we pull out one of the quarters, we can see silver—heads, tails, right side up, upside down, all around. We are fully forgiven, loved, and of high value to our Lord and Savior Yeshua (Jesus). When we pull out the second quarter, our testimony of the Lord is to defend others as well, especially when someone is being slandered. We simply agree with the truth from the perspective of Yeshua (Jesus). Part of the truth is not enough to vindicate the character of another.

The truth may well be that we or someone we know has sinned a grievous sin or committed several sins, but this is still just part of the truth. The rest of the truth is that this same someone who sinned is every bit as much forgiven, loved, and highly valued and has the potential of becoming a new creature created in Yeshua (Jesus) as we are. When someone is being belittled, we defend that same person with the knowledge of the Lord in how He sees a person. Yeshua (Jesus) did not die for our sins alone but also for the sins of the whole world.

The agape love of Yeshua (Jesus) in the shedding of His blood is what covers a multitude of sins. When the sins of others are being confessed, which is part of the truth, we bring in the rest of the truth by saying and agreeing with Yeshua (Jesus) that He is faithful and just to forgive. The same is true of us when our own character is being slandered.

When sins of our past are being brought up, we agree with the whole truth—the whole truth being that we are now new creatures in Yeshua (Jesus) created in Messiah (Christ) for good works.

Draw a thermometer, and mark on it the place that represents how well you can bless (say something good about) a person being slandered, including yourself.

Now, let's move on to prayer.

## *For Small Groups

Give everyone an opportunity to discuss blessing those who curse.

o   How do you manage to speak well of those who speak ill of you?

o   What guards do you have in place so as not to bite and devour another person in retaliation?

o   Are you aware of when you need to part company before saying something hurtful?

o   How do you deal with envy, your own or that of others?

o   How well equipped are you to deal with people when they bring up your past or the past of others?

# Chapter 23

# This Thing Called Prayer

We have arrived at the place of prayer. Before beginning, we need a working biblical definition of what prayer is and what it is not.

Prayer is agreeing with God and what He wants to come to pass and or come into our lives and the lives of others. We are agreeing with God that His will be done in our lives and the lives of others. Prayer does not always include what we want. We find this principle in action when Yeshua (Jesus) was praying in the garden: "Not my will but Thy will be done." Prayer does not always embody what others want. Prayer may not include what others want for us.

We discover this attitude prevalent when Yeshua (Jesus) rebuked Peter when He said, "Get behind me, Satan! Your interests are on man's interests, not on God's." What Yeshua (Jesus) was explaining to Peter is that interests for himself and for others such as Yeshua (Jesus) were not the same as the desires of God. Peter didn't want Yeshua (Jesus) to get crucified because he loved Yeshua (Jesus). Peter also did not want to lose someone he loved, which indicated love for himself. Peter was not in agreement with what God wanted in the life of Yeshua (Jesus).

Once we discover this truth, we can stand and agree with what God wants to come into our lives and the lives of others. God will honor those prayers.

There is another aspect of prayer we need to understand. God needs to have precedence over our prayer life. With an interrelationship between the

Lord and ourselves, Yeshua (Jesus) can and will become Lord over our prayer lives. Consider the following story to illustrate.

This story takes place after the life of a woman in her thirties ended up in chaos at the hands of two people who had at one time been close to her. Her earlier frame of mind was before she entered the Town of Igloos to learn the areas she needed help with in her life. Her story also began before she learned lessons in the city hall office of "Too Angry." She began reading about praying for specific people who had brought a great deal of pain into her life. In Luke 6:28(b), instructions are given to pray for those who mistreat you (us).

The woman was compliant to the instruction given by Yeshua (Jesus); however, her prayers were not God honoring. Her prayer life went something like this: "Yes, I'll pray for them. I'll pray that a truck runs over them. I'll pray that they experience a tenth of the pain I've suffered, and it won't be enough!" The woman heard the Lord ask, "Are you aware the prayers you uttered are not praying *for* them but *against* them? Do you know the prayers you prayed will hurt people I love if they come to pass?" She answered, "Yes." Then He asked, "What kind of prayers do you think need to be requested to prevent the pain you suffered from spreading?" With this final question, Yeshua (Jesus) became Lord of the prayer life of the woman.

How did this woman's story finish? She was sitting at home when she was urged to pray. She prayed that the Lord would intervene and change the mind of the person she was praying for. She asked the Lord to remove the desire to harm someone in order to get what he thought he needed. She asked for the Lord to give the man what he needed. After at least an hour of prayer, the woman realized she no longer wanted pain or sin to spread. She prayed for healing instead. She prayed for protection against the pain's spreading. She prayed for the Lord to bless him in his health, prosperity, and strength in his relationships with God, himself, and others.

Those kinds of prayers were lining up with what God wanted in the life of the man the woman was praying for. Let it be done here on earth as it is in heaven for the life of the man she prayed for. I do not know what has happened in the lives of individuals who have been hurt by others. I do know that those of us hurt by others can give our prayer lives to God and, in so doing, as much as it depends on us, stop sin from spreading through prayer.

The great part of praying for others is that every individual knows exactly what to pray for to prevent pain and sin from spreading. God gets the victory.

By the time this much of our journey has been completed, the temperatures of forgiveness, agape loving of others, doing good, blessing when cursed, and praying for people who have hurt us is now around sixty-five to seventy-five degrees Fahrenheit. When struggling with prayer, we can ask someone else to intercede until we are able.

Draw a thermometer, and mark the place that represents how well equipped you are at praying for your enemies.

Transformation is part of our destination as our journey comes to an end.


**\*For Small Groups**

Give participants an opportunity to discuss some methods unique to each individual when praying for their enemies.

- o What thoughts come to mind when we are instructed to pray for our enemies?

- o Has anyone struggled with prayers not lining up with what God wants in someone's life?

- o What would God need to reveal for Him to become Lord of your prayer life?

- o Does the idea of stopping sin from spreading help guide your prayer life?

# Chapter 24

## Transformed in Yeshua (Jesus)

We have completed our travels. The time has come to bring together all our thermometers. As we examine them and the marks we placed on them, look how far we have come on our journeys.

The marks are indicators pointing to areas of our lives that may need loving care as well as showing where we have grown. At the beginning of our journeys, did any of us conceive that we would not only forgive someone but also agape love, do good, bless, and pray for the very people who brought pain into our lives?

Yet here we are. We did not arrive here by accident. We are given a promise.

We will end our travels with the statement in Philippians 1:6(b): "He who began a good work in you will complete it until the day of Messiah (Christ) Yeshua (Jesus)."

Blessings and happy travels to you.

# Conclusion

Many people are often surprised to discover the truths that resulted in the effort of completing *A Journey to Forgiveness*.

Consider, for instance, both what the scripture does and does not say concerning this sensitive subject. The instructions written were penned after the death and resurrection of Yeshua (Jesus). The exhortation to put away unhealthy perceptions and hold on to wholesome emotions informs us as believers that we have God-given abilities to forgive through the assistance of the Holy Spirit.

An enjoyable aspect of this book is the number of Christians discovering for themselves that they possess not only the ability to forgive but also the ability to surpass forgiveness. *A Journey to Forgiveness* is written for any individual; however, the book is also designed for discussion and growth in small groups where journeys can be shared. The book is intended to reveal truths and uncover myths surrounding the subject of forgiveness. The writing challenges Christian growth with pleasant outcomes as chapter after chapter unfolds. We can come to understand the order of emotions and why certain emotions precede feelings we are to embrace.

As a case in point, why do instructions to put away emotions such as unhealthy anger, wrath, and so on come before the teaching to have a heart of compassion, kindness, and forgiveness toward ourselves and others? What does the Word "all" contain within it? We as Christians do not have to determine whether or not we are to forgive those who have sinned against us. We know we are instructed to do so. Often the predicament we find ourselves in is *how* to forgive. *A Journey to Forgiveness* offers specific outlines that address this very quandary. The book does not make light of intense emotions such as bitterness but rather shows how to express and deal with them in a healthy environment. *A Journey to Forgiveness* helps us comprehend and apply the Word of God through the simple metaphor of taking a trip.

In the beginning, our excursion is pleasant. As time goes by and travel continues, we are suddenly caught in a snowstorm. The snowstorm eventually lands many of us right in front of an avalanche that may block our way to forgiveness. Good news is on the horizon as we learn how to move the avalanche out of our way and continue to our destination. At times, we may find ourselves stuck in certain emotions that slow down or prohibit forgiveness. We learn about areas where we may feel stuck, recognize these areas when we are, and discover how to get the necessary help in order to continue. The book is written in a teaching style that is easy to grasp. *A Journey to Forgiveness* assists in excelling in the areas of agape loving, doing good, blessing, and praying for our enemies.

For many people, learning and understanding how to walk in forgiveness is a difficult thing to accomplish. After speaking with several people about forgiveness, I realize they are acutely aware that there is more to forgiveness than just saying the words "I forgive you" when at the end of the day, these same people continue to be plagued with anger or bitterness. Ephesians and Colossians instruct us to put away unhealthy anger and embrace healthy emotions. There are purposes for those instructions. One is so that joy (fruit of the Spirit) can be embraced as part of life once again.

Another even larger goal is to bring the agape love of Yeshua (Jesus) to persons desperately needing His forgiveness. He accomplishes His task through each one of us.

# About the Author

Idaho native Cindy Skimming attended Wenatchee Valley College in Washington but attributes much of her personal and spiritual growth to her experiences after becoming a believer in 2003 and studying the works of Beth Moore and Joyce Meyer. After relocating to Utah, Skimming received training through the Christian Disciplines Institute, where she completed training in leadership principles such as the cost of leadership, doctrine, and Christian maturity, and the essential qualities of leadership. Skimming's studies ultimately led to the publication of A Journey to Forgiveness.

Skimming is on fire for God and lives to serve Him in practical ways. Her imagination runs wild in the boundless joy of discovering new ways to bless those she encounters. She's passionate about God's message of mercy and prays that her readers find the tangible love of Yeshua in her work and allow it to open their own hearts to the power of forgiveness.

www.ingramcontent.com/pod-product-compliance
Lightning Source LLC
LaVergne TN
LVHW051102080426
835508LV00019B/2011